MW00583862

DIVINE FEMININE ENERGY

*How To Manifest With Goddess Energy & Feminine
Energy Awakening Secrets They Don't Want You To Know
About (Manifesting For Women & Feminine Energy
Awakening 2 In 1 Collection)*

ANGELA GRACE

Ascending Vibrations

CONTENTS

PART II
FEMININE ENERGY AWAKENING
GODDESS ENERGY SECRETS & HOW TO
STEP INTO YOUR DIVINE POWER

GET YOUR *BONUS*
MANIFESTING SECRET FORMULA
TOOLKIT

Are you DONE with settling for a mediocre life, wasting precious time, & ready to live your wildest fantasies?

- Hack your brain, boost performance, & release blocks holding you back from greatness
- Awaken this amazing energy to supercharge your manifestations
- Stop wasting what little precious time you have on ineffective methods

I. **Supercharged Manifestation EFT Tapping Video**
Download To Banish Limiting Beliefs & Propel You Toward Your Dream Life! (Infused with 432 Hz Frequency)

1. **Secret Formula Journal!** Daily manifestation Ritual Done For You, Simply Rinse & Repeat At Home! (You Can Print This Out, Stick On Your Wall, & Cross Off The Days You Complete The Ritual)

1. **Powerful 10 Minute 'Shifting Your reality' Guided Meditation** MP3 Download (Infused with 528 Hz Frequency)

1. ***BONUS*** LOA boosting 10 Minute 'Feminine Energy Awakening' Guided Meditation MP3 Download

Go To This Link To Get Your *BONUS* Manifesting Secret Formula Toolkit:

bit.ly/manifestingforwomen

PLEASE LEAVE A REVIEW ON AMAZON

From the bottom of my heart, thank you for reading my book. I truly hope that it helps you on your spiritual journey and to live a more empowered and happy life. If it does help you, then I'd like to ask you for a favor. Would you be kind enough to leave an honest review for this book on Amazon? It'd be greatly appreciated and will likely impact the lives of other spiritual seekers across the globe, giving them hope and power. I read **every** review I receive and they help me to become the best writer and spiritual teacher that I can be.

Thank you and good luck!

Angela Grace

Why not join our Facebook community and discuss your spiritual path with like-minded seekers?

We would love to hear from you!

Go here to join the 'Ascending Vibrations' community:

bit.ly/ascendingvibrations

❧ I ❧
MANIFESTING FOR WOMEN

Speed Abundance, Why the Law of Attraction
Is Not Working, & How to Manifest With
Divine Feminine Energy

INTRODUCTION

I am extremely glad that you have landed on this book, dear ladies! Let me welcome you to a sublime world filled with wonders and amazing things ahead. Manifesting is a magnificent tool: as long as you know how to use it. With that in mind, I hope my book gives you not only the inspiration to move forward but also offers you all the information you need to optimize your manifesting performance. In the chapters below, you are going to find step-by-step guidelines about how to perform your manifestations in a way that flows all the positive energy towards you.

Many women are exactly like you—trying to figure out how they can attract all the things they have been craving for into their lives. Even though it might sound easy, you have found the hard way that life is much more than meets the eye. It is most likely that you have already tried to practice manifesting along with other spiritual activities that would bring you closer to your goal. Yet, the results have been much less impressive than what you have anticipated. Why is that? Well, I can tell you right now that by reading through this book, you will identify all these minor setbacks. By doing so, you can rest assured that your manifesting experience will become a lot more exciting and fruitful.

I understand the skepticism as I myself have doubted the power of the universe. I did not realize how my energy affected my reality. Are you doing the same thing: drowning in negative thoughts and expecting something to miraculously take place? You should not get disappointed as true changes cannot happen overnight. They take time and effort. You need to be patient, and allow the universe to work its magic. If you are looking for abundance, then this is what you are going to receive. Let it go, and detach from that persistent thought. This will prevent you from overcharging yourself with unmet expectations. There are no alarm clocks, no time frames, and no deadlines.

Through this book, you will learn a lot about how the Law of Attraction works. Unlike what many people believe, this is not just a gimmick or a trend that has gathered temporary attention until it fades away again. On the contrary, it is a shift in your mindset that is based on a whole philosophical system, and is backed by science. How awesome is that? Two entirely different ways of looking at how things merge and set the foundations of this great tool. Use the Law of Attraction, and you can shape your life in the way you have always wanted. It sounds unbelievable, but I promise you it is the truth.

Starting out without filling the gaps, and truly understanding the meaning of manifesting will not do you any good; in fact, it can even derail you from your initial purpose. Instead, follow the structure that I have included here in my book. Read through the chapters, and keep notes. Organize your mind, and prepare yourself for an extraordinary experience. When you are ready to let that positive energy flow right through you, begin your manifestations. As you see yourself transforming into who you really want to be, as you see the world around you offer you everything you have been dreaming of in the past, you will look back on this moment and be grateful.

Below, you will find my personal journey, as well as a detailed outline of what you are about to read in this book. I hope it helps you fuel your motivation, and inspires you to get that inspirational juice flowing.

MY PERSONAL MANIFESTING JOURNEY

Before we begin this marvelous journey towards manifesting, allow me to share some information about myself. I am experienced in energy healing, Reiki, and crystals. I discovered the power of crystals, energy healing, and spirituality after being introduced to that by my friend, Linda. I am so grateful for her insight and her kindness towards me. This has opened up a whole new world for me, filled with potentials I never even knew existed.

Personally, I have never pictured myself devoted to the spiritual world. In fact, I would even end up mocking those who believed in a higher power. Oh boy, was I wrong! In my life, I have been through various ups and downs; I am guessing most of you can relate to that. No matter how hard I tried, I could not catch a break. After three years of hard work and exhaustion from sleep deprivation, I found myself on the verge of being broke. I felt depressed and unable to enjoy anything in life. What was the point of working so hard if this did not offer me anything in return? I was completely shocked, and honestly, I did not know where to turn to for help.

Linda convinced me to try manifesting. She explained briefly what the Law of Attraction was, and at first I was very skeptical. However, the more she spoke about it, the more it made sense. Maybe this was keeping me away from my goals and dreams. My energy was not aligned to the universe: it felt like a complete revelation. My eyes were wide open, and I literally soaked in every single word she said about energy healing, inner balance, meditation, and everything in between.

I started doing my own research, and gradually reached a point where I could communicate with my spiritual self. In time, I discovered my divine feminine energy, and suddenly my whole world changed. My life transformed—I invited abundance, love, and happiness. No longer did I have to worry about this negativism that spread its shadows over me. I felt better than ever before, and I thank the universe for making that happen.

To this day, I am proud to have written some truly inspirational books that I share with the rest of the world. "Energy Made Easy," "Protect Your Energy," Crystals Made Easy," "Feminine Energy Awakening," and "Reiki Made Easy," are books that have sprung out of my desire to share my journey. I take delight in shedding some light into that knowledge, as I am well aware of the impact it might have on a person's life. Join me in my path, and experience what the universe can do for you!

Are You Ready?

In this book, I am going to discuss what manifesting actually is. Along with the philosophical background, I am also going to help you understand the basics behind the science of vibrational frequencies. Only through this knowledge can you fully grasp the meaning of aligning your energy to that of the universe. Moving on, I will introduce you to several techniques used around the world for increasing your vibrational frequency. Techniques such as EFT, TRE, and hypnosis can contribute greatly to your goal.

Of course, nothing would happen without the divine feminine energy. Therefore, I have dedicated a whole chapter discussing this raw force and how to awaken it from within. The Law of Dharma is another amazing concept, and you will love the seven spiritual laws of success that I have included here. Next, I have focused on love, and how to manifest a loving relationship in your life. You can either set your mind on your ex, or invite a totally new person in your life for a great experience. Later in the book, I will be explaining how certain tools amplify your energy, and maximize the benefits you get out of the process. Visual boards, scripting, positive affirmations, and templates to turn to: these are all elements that will help you structure your manifesting routine.

There are obviously guided meditations available in this book, as well as some hacks to decrease the time frame, in which you can expect your manifesting to come true. I have also referred to some of the most common obstacles that you might encounter throughout your spiritual journey, along with effective ways to overcome those barriers. Finally, I have created a powerful daily ritual that enhances your manifestations. I am sure that you are super excited to read this book. Are you ready to set out on this once-in-a-lifetime adventure?

INTRODUCTION TO
MANIFESTING FOR WOMEN

I guess you have heard about the Law of Attraction at some point in your life. Maybe some of you are skeptical as to whether it is a real thing. Well, to tell you the truth, it is all a matter of physics. The Law of Attraction pretty much resembles the law of gravity. When you let something fall down to the ground from a higher point, then it inevitably falls. There is no question about it since gravity attracts it to the ground: unless you are in space, of course. So, in a similar pattern, your body seems to attract exactly what you have been thinking of.

Let me elaborate a little on that particular process. Your body is filled with energy, vibrating at a pace your mind dictates. You may feel this energy, or you might ignore its presence. In any case, it is omnipresent. So this particular vibration of your body is what attracts certain things to come your way. The biggest challenge is for you to identify how to attract the pleasant things in life. Many people end up attracting everything they have been trying to avoid in the first place. So is this all random?

Luckily, you have control over what you attract. You simply need to figure out how to channel your desires. It all takes place in your mind. Divided into two distinct categories, your conscious and subconscious mind both work their magic nonstop. Ever since you are born, your subconscious gets filled with the stimuli you get. This is where all the memories are formed, along with your habits. In fact, the environment shapes who you are—it shapes your paradigm. All these pieces of information you gather are collected in your subconscious mind, creating who you ultimately become.

On the other hand, your conscious mind is responsible for your thoughts. These are all in alignment with what you receive from the environment. For instance, you see something that makes you sad, and then you think about how to make things right. It is fascinating that, most likely, your thoughts will be in harmony with your subconscious. The two distinct parts of your mind are, in essence, communicating vessels. Your conscious mind thinks in a specific way, which triggers your subconscious mind. Then, your subconscious mind dictates the vibrating energy in your body. Does that make sense to you?

Many people misinterpret the Law of Attraction. They believe it only takes a shift in the way they think in order to benefit from all these amazing things in their lives: if only things were that easy. Nevertheless, it is necessary to dig deeper. If you are really determined to change the course of your life, you need to aim at your subconscious mind. This is where you control your emotions. No matter how hard you try to change your thinking process, the result will stay the same. It goes without even saying that you should try to put aside any hesitation, and step out of your comfort zone. Try to understand what has contributed to forming your emotional mind the way you have so that you can modify it. Be careful, because this is not going to happen overnight. It takes a lot of effort and hard work to achieve something like that. But, at the end of the day, it is all so worth it.

Below, I am going to show you exactly where the problem lies. You might have tried to live by the principles dictated within the Law of Attraction but you have found it hard to do so. However, you need to fully comprehend the basics before you are ready to embark on that wonderful journey: one step at a time. First, we need to understand the science behind the Law of Attraction. Is there really any relevant scientific evidence backing the power of positive thinking? In a nutshell, there is. It all boils down to quantum physics.

UNDERSTANDING THE SCIENCE OF FREQUENCIES

Quantum physics sounds difficult to grasp, right? It might even appear to be intimidating. Yet, understanding the science will unveil the great mysteries of the universe, allowing you to attract the things you want in your life. According to the Hertz Vibration Scale, each emotion reflects a different rate of vibration. Starting at very low frequencies, there are emotions such as shame, anger, guilt, fear, and apathy. As you move up the ladder, you will find emotions like acceptance, love, joy, peace, and enlightenment (Smith, 2018).

This chart indicates that your body's vibration changes, depending on what you feel. Can you imagine that? If you feel guilt all the time, your body's vibration will be low. Therefore, it is inescapable to attract negative things in your life. You cannot help but stay in the same vicious cycle. Or can you? Fortunately, you can change the way you feel. As a result, you will gradually start attracting the proper things that you should experience. Why send out a bad signal in order to receive an identical signal that will only prolong your misery?

Now that you have comprehended the way your body sends and receives signals—resembling radio or TV in a way—it is time to move forward. "How can I use Quantum Physics tools to attract what I really want?"—this is a question that must be popping up in your mind a lot. Well, there are tools that you can use. First and foremost, you need to increase the vibrating frequency you emit. It sounds simple enough, does it not? Unless you understand how you are able to do so, though, it is not going to be consistent. There are many ways allowing you to accomplish that increase in your body's vibrations. The most common of them all include laughter, meditation, and workout.

What you should understand about frequencies is that everything in the universe has one. Nevertheless, there is a special frequency for every little thing in the world that allows that particular thing to perform at its peak. Does that make sense? This is called a resonant frequency and defines the point when something reaches its highest level of oscillation. You understand that everything is vibration: the moment you realize the specific vibration you ought to reach for making the most out of your manifestation, you have what it takes to proceed. With that knowledge in mind, you can never fail in your endeavors.

Another helpful tool is to realize how you feel. Rather than rejecting all the negative emotions, you should first analyze them. Awareness is the first step towards improvement: you cannot have one without the other. Find out the reasons why you are sad, disappointed, or filled with guilt. Rationalize these emotions and then let them go. Aim high at the Hertz Vibration Scale, overflowing with emotions that make you vibrate a lot more. Obviously, you cannot force yourself to love someone. You cannot force yourself to enjoy a specific recreational activity. It should come from within. Hence, what you need to do is figure out what makes your heart skip a beat. What makes you happy is key to attracting happiness. This might sound self-explanatory; however, most people tend to follow a different path in their life, ending up miserable. Find your true colors, and wear them with pride. If there is something your heart is aching to pursue, do not ignore that desire.

It is equally important to surround yourself with people that make you feel good. Their energy is going to lift you up instead of bringing you down all the time. I know that all people come with their special baggage. Sometimes it is their family dragging them down, a toxic relationship, a needy friend. Nevertheless, do you really want to sacrifice your well-being just to avoid confrontation? Are you willing to put your own hopes and dreams on hold purely to continue being poisoned by the toxic presence of those around you? I do not think so! Embrace the people who emit at a high vibrational scale in order to benefit from their positive lifestyle. You will be amazed at the results.

Last but definitely not least, you have to make sure that your mind is set for success. In other words, failure should be eliminated from your dictionary. Failing is not an option. You need to believe in your power and be 100% confident in what you deserve. This is the only way for you to claim what you are entitled to, instead of constantly compromising your desires, your feelings, and your ambitions. It is essential that your mind understands that—your happiness is non-negotiable. Once you realize that deep in your very core, you will feel your vibration elevating. It is pure physics, I am telling you!

Attracting What You Truly Want in Life

Backed by scientific research, the Law of Attraction dictates that positive thinking is essential towards receiving abundance and happiness in life. Ji Young Jung et al have proven that positive thinking has led to increased life satisfaction in life, which is a groundbreaking assumption (Jung et al., 2007). Indeed, it is great to know that your own mind can affect your well-being. There is a strong correlation between the way you feel and the course of your life. If you spend every waking hour complaining and feeling miserable, then you must be sure that your situation is never going to change. Shift your mindset in order to welcome joy in your life. This is science talking, not just me!

If you can dream it, then you can be it. Although it does sound like an advertising motto, the truth is that visualization is deeply rooted to successful outcomes. Where would we be without dreaming, after all? When you want something, you must do everything within your power to achieve that. This means changing the way you feel about yourself, so as to let physics work in your favor. Start emitting high vibration frequencies in order to attract the results that you have been waiting to see in your life. Do not rely on luck or randomness. Do not wait until the stars align and "fate" performs its miracles. Be the master of your own life, and lead it exactly where you want to go.

Let us get back to scientific evidence, which supports the theory behind the Law of Attraction. There are neurological structures, which are called mirror neurons. These structures were primarily found in monkeys, but scientists have interpreted similar ones in the human

ANGELA GRACE

neurological system. According to the research conducted at the University of Parma, mirror neurons are responsible for beings imitating the behavioral patterns that they observe around them. This means that behavior tends to be imitated, depending on proximity (Jaffe, 2011).

If you are angry, you will most likely notice that those around you imitate that particular behavior. This will happen even if they do not know what has made you angry in the first place. They will sense and pick up on this negative energy, mirroring it to their own self. You will be affected by other people's behavior, of course. In your surroundings, you must have felt that you get influenced by how others feel and they do the same. Mirror neurons contribute to that effect, explaining why this happens to a great extent. We basically exchange energy, becoming aligned to those who are close to us (Jaffe, 2011).

Finally, it is worth considering the fact that intention and action stem from the very same parts of the brain. As a consequence, whenever we stimulate the parts of the brain responsible for what we intend to do, we basically stimulate those parts of the brain that trigger our actions (Gollwitzer & Sheeran, 2006). How does that sound? In this way, it is important to strengthen our visualization of what we want to achieve. Sooner or later, our brain will interpret this visualization as something that needs to be made a reality. There are of course tools that can help you towards enhancing your intentions, basically channeling your desires in a way that enables you to make them come true.

As you can see, there is much more than what meets the eye in the Law of Attraction. Behavior can be interpreted scientifically, offering solid proof that it works. It is worth changing your life by learning the mechanisms that are able to provide for you what you have been dreaming of all this time. Instead of feeling sad that you have not met your goals just yet, get excited about the future ahead of you. This is going to be a bright future, filled with joy and abundance. It is a magical journey that has only just begun. Are you excited to hop on that train, waving farewell to your past insecurity and sorrow?

12

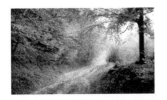

MANIFESTING YOUR DREAM
VERSION OF YOURSELF

The Law of Attraction is absolutely feasible, as long as it starts from within. You must reprogram your mind so as to believe in the new "you" before you are able to manifest it to the world. As you will find out the hard way, the heaviest barrier is placed in front of you by your very own set of beliefs. It is your mindset that has been holding you back, surrounding you with negative energy. Do you really want to remain like that? Do you want to sacrifice your dream version of yourself, simply because you have been accustomed to less?

We should face it: the world is a mirror. The mirror reflects only what you place in front of it. Well, the same happens with your life. If you drown yourself in negative thoughts, fears, and doubts, this is what you are bound to encounter in your life. The same things, over and over again. Unless you do something about it, things will never change. You cannot spend your life waiting for someone else to take charge, and save you from your misery. Why would you do that? You are holding the key to unlock literally anything you have ever dreamed of in life.

It is important to understand that you create the limitations in your daily life, and you are responsible for lifting them altogether.

Otherwise, you will be stuck in a never-ending ordeal. Embrace yourself, and believe that you are worthy of love, wealth, and prosperity. There is a widespread misconception that modesty is the right way to go. As a result, most people tend to avoid praising their inner self. They decrease the value of their accomplishments, and they avoid talking about their strengths: do not fall for that trap. If you diminish your value, others will just think the same. After all, this is what you are going to attract.

Limiting beliefs are the number one culprit preventing you from reaching your dream self. Once you identify them, you need to work hard and eventually eliminate them. Why waste your time self-loathing, when you can conquer greatness? Why would you ever settle for anything less than the life you deserve? It is essential that you realize what the beliefs are in order to fight them off once and for all. You should not let anyone, including yourself, prevent you from walking your special path in life.

Building confidence is of paramount importance here. Allow others to see who you truly are, as the version you have been dreaming of all this time. Stay focused and true to yourself, never missing even the slightest opportunity to shine. I know that at first this will sound opposite to what you have grown up to believe. It has always been the norm to avoid bragging. However, you ought to be aware of your greatness. You need to be 100% confident in your powers in order for others to believe the same. In this way, the Law of Attraction will work in your favor.

In case you are wondering how to achieve that, it takes a lot of time and dedication. There is no more room for self-doubt. No more letting others define who you are. You are a strong, independent individual; you are worthy of love, abundance, success, wealth, and every other thing that you have set your mind on to accomplish. Some great tools that can come in handy for you feature scripting and positive affirmations. Try using a journal, where you clearly write down what you think of yourself. Why are you proud of who you are and what you want to become? Then, use these affirmations in order to cultivate that positive feeling inside you. Nourish your mind with the dream version of yourself, so that you project it to the world and attract it right back.

Obviously, there are several techniques that can help you reach your manifesting goals more efficiently. Among them, you can try out Emotional Freedom Technique (EFT tapping), Trauma Release Exercises (TRE), and self-hypnosis. These tools will enable you to elevate your body's vibration frequencies, getting closer to your target of experiencing the Law of Attraction to its fullest potential.

THE WONDERFUL VIBE OF EFT TAPPING

Have you ever wished you could hack into your brain, boosting your performance? Have you ever wondered if there is a way to optimize your mind's function, modifying what you believe has been holding you back from achieving greatness? I hate to be the bearer of bad news, but the truth is your brain does not come with a detailed manual. If it did, you could study every single page and eventually learn how to tame it. However, there are several techniques out there doing the exact same thing. One of these techniques is EFT, or else tapping. According to EFT, you can change your vibration frequency through gently tapping specific parts of your body. In this way, you can affect your energy and attract equally elevated frequencies in your life (Anthony, 2017).

EFT focuses on the meridian points on your body, therefore resembling acupuncture quite often. While you are tapping the external part of your palm, the third eye on your forehead, your cheeks, or the top of your head, you are encouraged to repeat positive affirmations about yourself. Although at first you might feel awkward doing so, you will immediately experience a boost in your spirit. As you progress with the technique, you will notice that your mental clarity skyrockets. You feel less physical pain and your mood certainly improves.

Below, I am going to guide you through two very simple, yet absolutely brilliant, step-by-step EFT tapping sessions. The first one targets letting go of your limiting beliefs, while the second enables you to attract what it is you have been eager to attract.

Release Limiting Beliefs

It can be hard to deal with your long-lasting beliefs which keep bringing you down instead of lifting you up to where you want to go. It is true that most of us cling on to such beliefs, often sabotaging our course of life. We feel incapable of changing, always returning to the same patterns: it is a slippery slope which we must avoid at all costs. In order to do that, we first need to identify these limiting beliefs. Then, after knowing what we are up against, we will focus on reversing the situation.

First of all, I would like you to close your eyes. Think of a negative, limiting belief. It can be anything, like your conviction that you are not good enough to succeed, or your fear of confronting others. You might see yourself as a lazy person, an individual lacking in educational background, or as a person who does not deserve to be loved. Pick the one thing that causes the biggest discomfort for you. Now, take a deep breath and repeat the following: "I am a lazy person, but I accept that. I love myself despite that." How does that make you feel?

After having done that, start tapping the external part of your palm, saying the exact same thing. Then, move forward with the area in between your eyebrows. Start repeating what you think you are, but this time focus on your actions. Specifically, focus on the actions that contradict your accusation. For example, if you consider yourself lazy, think of all the times when you have proved yourself wrong. All these hard workouts, the times when you had completed a project in time, or the endless days of studying. Continue tapping, this time moving your fingers right next to your eyes. Afterwards, move below the eyes and on your cheekbones.

Tapping is a wonderful way to relax. Tap your chin, and then right above your upper lip. Continue repeating that the specific opinion of yourself is mistaken. Now, start tapping both sides of your chest. You will feel an invigorating sensation slowly overwhelming you. Use positive affirmations, so as to believe deep inside yourself that you do not deserve to be categorized as a lazy person. Tap the area below your arms and then take another deep breath. If you try to repeat your initial belief, you will feel a lot lighter. Try doing the same routine for a week, and you will be amazed at the results.

Attract What You Want

In a similar pattern, you will need to reinforce your belief that what you want actually wants you. This is a very strong feeling, and you should be truly confident to achieve that. First, tap on the external part of your palm with four fingers. Start saying positive affirmations, like the following: "I choose to believe that what I want wants me. I love and cherish myself. Moreover, I respect who I am. I honor myself." Move on to your third eye, repeating the same things: "I love myself, and I know that I am worthy of accepting what I want. It is already on its way, and I have faith in myself."

After the third eye, move below the eyes. Then, tap your upper lip area and your chin. Repeat similar affirmations, which are going to make you feel better: "I know that what I want is available to me. I open myself to receive it." Then, tap your throat and the area below your arm. Once you are done, start over. Start tapping the third eye again, acknowledging that you have been holding back to receiving what you want: "I choose to believe that I have resisted what I want. I am now open to receiving that. I am not holding back any longer."

When you are feeling good enough, start tapping on the top of your head, repeating the following: "I am feeling about the fact that what I want wants me back, and I am ready to receive that in my life." This affirmation is the perfect way to end this session. Enjoy the same session as often as you need to, in order to open yourself up to new possibilities.

Trauma Release Exercises & Self-Hypnosis

Negative energy keeps us at a low frequency. Whatever keeps you at a stressed state prevents you from actually experiencing the benefits deriving from the Law of Attraction. In order to open yourself to the wonderful effects of elevated frequencies, you need to deal with any underlying issues from the past. Face it: the past can be overwhelming. It can be daunting, creeping its way without us even realizing. However, there are ways to settle the score, bury the hatchet, and come to peace with our past traumas. One excellent technique used to release the tension caused by stress is TRE.

TRE stands for Tension and Trauma Release Exercises. It is actually a natural method, which you can see in the animal kingdom if you pay attention to the signs. When you see a dog feeling scared about an imminent threat, you will most likely notice that it starts shaking. Through this repetitive move, the dog releases its tension. Thus, shaking can help restore the balance in frequency within your own body. Your body is more relaxed, vibrating in a positive manner (Emma Claire Donovan, 2019).

You can practice TRE simply by putting pressure on specific muscles on your body. One fine example would be to lean against a wall as you are standing upright, touching the wall with your back. Start slow, opening your legs a little. Act like you are trying to sit down, gently lowering your body and bending your knees. Once you feel your leg muscles burn, hold the position. Gradually, you will notice that your legs are starting to shake. Push as much as you want, without causing discomfort.

Alternatively, you can lie down on your back. Whatever makes you feel more at ease. Bend your knees, so that your feet are touching the ground. Now, try to lift your torso and hips a little. Your legs will start burning, and eventually, you will start shaking. If you feel that the shaking experience is too much, then stop. Stretch and become aware of the process. Repeat the same session over and over again, enjoying the therapeutic release of tension. These soothing tremors will allow you to get rid of the excess energy. In many cases, this is stagnant energy that has been kept into your body all this time.

Once you are fully relaxed, you can turn to self-hypnosis for manifesting your desires. This is another immensely useful tool, which allows you to broaden your horizons. Self-hypnosis is something you can do on your own from the comfort of your own home. Nestled in your shelter, you are free to expand yourself, open up to new experiences, and receive the gifts you have been meant to receive all along in your life. Create a relaxing atmosphere by choosing soft music in the background, scented candles, and a cozy room. Sit comfortably in a chair or on the sofa. Wear something light and look up at the ceiling.

Of course, it goes without even saying that you need to pay attention to the temperature, as well as any other detail that might stand in the way. For instance, if you are feeling extremely hot, you cannot get into a state of hypnosis. The heat will distract you from achieving that nothingness in order to let go of your conscious mind. The same happens if there are constant noises all around you. Make sure that you are able to devote time to hypnosis before moving on with the session.

It is best to do that when you are alone at home or at least when you can have your personal space available to you without any distractions.

Focus on your breathing as you repeat to yourself that you are very tired: you want to sleep. After a few minutes, you will notice your muscles letting go. Breathe in and out slowly, enjoying the silence and absolute harmony all around. As you become familiar with self-hypnosis, you will start adding positive affirmations in this section. You will repeat in your mind the things that you want to achieve in life. What do you want to attract? Picture these things in vivid colors. Be as detailed as you like, concentrating on the conviction that you are on your way to eventually attract all that and more. When you are ready to come back, start counting from one to five. Do not rush it—instead, take your time and become aware of the surroundings.

The first time you practice self-hypnosis might feel a little awkward. After regaining consciousness, you may feel lightheaded. However, you will grow into this experience. After a few sessions, you will require a lot less time to balance between the conscious and the subconscious mind. Moreover, the benefits that you receive from hypnosis amplify as you stick with that pattern. Give it a try, and delve into the mysteries of what lies within you!

ACHIEVE ANYTHING BY AWAKENING YOUR DIVINE FEMININE ENERGY

A re you aware of the divine feminine energy within you? You have been blessed with a powerful force and you may not even know that. In my book *"Feminine Energy Awakening"* I have focused greatly on how every single one of us can awaken that precious energy. This is a life-changing process, which will open your mind to a whole new world. Rather than feeling trapped, unable to release this energy that has been boiling deep inside you, what you need to do is find a way to channel it. Bring it forward, and let it shower you with enlightenment. By doing so, you will see your life fully transformed and shaped exactly the way you have always pictured it to be.

You are a unique being, and you should not be ashamed of your uniqueness. Instead, you should embrace it. Only after having fully comprehended your greatness can you be expected to shine. It is a long process, involving deep soul searching. This is not going to be easy. There are many obstacles ahead, but in my book you will find all the helpful practical guidelines you need. These guidelines will pave the way for you to walk on, discovering your purpose in life. You need to release all the negative energy and become aligned with your own positive feelings. By opening your chakras, you will be able to reach your spiritual self. Through this experience of awakening your divine feminine energy, you will realize that you deserve to be loved and cherished.

This is not a contest of genders,as some might claim. There is no point in comparing the virtues of men or women. It is not a question of who is the best. In fact, there is no reason to get into such a conversation. It will distract you from your deeper purpose, which is to discover your higher self. How can you do that when there are heavy anchors of negative emotions dragging you down? Men and women should not antagonize one another; instead, they should show respect and work together to achieve greatness.

You are special: the sooner you realize that, the better it will be. When you focus on others, you stray from your path towards self-completion. Why would you do that to yourself? Your entity is divine. You are driven by the eternal power of feminine energy which allows you to fulfill your goals. This energy needs to be cherished and nurtured. Do not let others deprive you of that wonderful opportunity to reach new heights. Now is your time to prove your value and expose to the world what you can accomplish.

The divine feminine goddess energy is of exceptional importance, in order for you to reveal your unique personality. If you are determined to embody your timeless greatness, then you should focus on how to awaken that energy. Due to social standards, personal relationships, past traumas, and limitations posed to you by others, your divine energy has remained dormant. However, if you truly want to stand out, and reach out to your higher self, you need to release this power and reap the benefits.

THE ROLE OF DIVINE FEMININE GODDESS ENERGY

One of the key elements in your path to claiming all these wonderful things in life is to be in touch with your feminine energy. Unlike what many people believe, being feminine is not about gender. Take a moment and think about ancient Chinese philosophy. There is the symbol of Yin and Yang, which represents the opposites that coexist in an entity. In order to achieve balance, these opposites are equally important: life cannot be without them (Cartwright, 2018).

In modern society, much attention has been drawn to masculine characteristics. Even women have suppressed their own distinctive traits just because they wanted to fit in. Of course, masculinity can come with its perks. Logic is paramount along with determination, strong will, and fearlessness. However, an individual needs so much more. Where is the emotional wealth, the creativity, and the affection? This is where feminine characteristics come in to save the day. As you can see, every person needs to tread lightly between their feminine and masculine side. This is the only way to accomplish that precious balance in life.

Now, I am sure you have a clear picture in your mind about the way your masculine and feminine energy should work together. How can this be? Well, it is a matter of priorities. When you want to set a goal, you need to bring out the masculine energy of yours. So, before proceeding any further, this is what you should do. Organize everything, setting your goals in a viable plan. Determine the time frame in which you are expected to complete your goals. Stick to the plan, pushing it forward no matter what.

After having done all that, you have created a solid foundation. What is even more important, perhaps, is the ability to receive the good things that you have anticipated through your goal setting. This is time for your feminine energy to step in once more, in order to allow yourself to receive. What is it that you have been eager to get? Is it money, fame, personal growth, love, or affection? Open up your mind and be ready to embrace these amazing things. They might not come to you right away, but they will come. As long as your divine feminine goddess energy is in charge, you have nothing to fear.

Does that sound contradictory to you? Take a look at your business, for example. You have been assigned a very important project.

This project is time sensitive and it relies solely on your performance. If your masculine energy was always in charge, what would you do? You would set your goal to complete a project and then you would constantly push yourself. Do you think this would allow you to finish in time? Chances are that you would feel drained, and exhausted, lacking both energy and creativity. Sooner or later, you would crave for a change.

By taking a break, taking a power nap, or going out for a walk, you would relieve yourself from that constant pressure. After that small pause, your performance would definitely improve. Although continuing on your initial plan might have given you the reassurance that you were doing your best, the truth is far from it. What can you get out of this example? Sometimes, it is best to trust your intuition. There is no point in going to extremes simply because you think you will always cope with the challenges. Harder work is not always the answer. Sometimes, a feminine approach is much more effective in life.

Building trust around you is paramount. Without trust and faith, you cannot succeed in reaching your goals. How can you reach out to love unless you have faith that love is going to come your way? Although your intellect might dictate otherwise, you need to cultivate that trust, and sit still. By doing so, you allow yourself to receive the gift of love. If you kept moving, just like your masculine energy would have suggested, how could you receive love?

Unveiling the Power Within You

Now that you know how important it is for you to discover that hidden source of energy from within, it is time to figure out how to do so. I am sure you feel overwhelmed by the prospect of awakening such a powerful energy, in order to experience your true potential. How can you unravel the mystical force, and let it work its magic? Fortunately, there are many things that you can do. All these small changes in your life will add to becoming more conscious and getting into closer contact with your higher self.

First and forevermore, you should keep a journal. This will track your progress and show you how to move forward. It goes without even saying that it is a long process, and it takes time until you comprehend how your body, mind, and soul become fully aligned.

Through journaling, you can write down every single thing that has helped you in your day; at the same time, you can mention all the little things that have raised a barrier in your efforts. You will use the "trial and error" technique to explore what suits your own personalized needs more.

Then, it is important to heal your inner child. Get rid of all the conflicts, the complexes, and the past traumas: they prevent you from contacting your divine energy. Indisputably, you need to deal with what has happened in the past. If you do not, then you cannot anticipate all the marvelous benefits to be unfolded before your eyes. You must heal the wounds by addressing the issues and resolving them. Of course, this is a strenuous, and often challenging procedure. It needs to be completed, though, before you claim what you are entitled to by birth. How else could you move on with your life?

Positive affirmations will help you come to terms with your divine feminine energy. You can use them as a means to believe in your divinity. Even if at first these affirmations make you feel uncomfortable, you need to step it up, and accept who you are. There is no room for being modest. You are a unique being, and you ought to believe that before reaching the point in your life where you are showered by your divine feminine energy. So, start boosting your self-esteem through numbering your great qualities. You will soon see that you deserve everything.

Along with acknowledging your value, you should also be thankful for what you already have. Count your blessings, and give thanks for the people around you. Be thankful for your health and all the opportunities that have come your way so far. You must realize that life is filled with gifts, and you have already been given a lot. Take a moment to think about it. Maybe you have been blessed with a loving partner or happy children. Perhaps you have skyrocketed your career. Your friends, and acquaintances, and your social network are also people you should be grateful for, unless you feel they are toxic. In that case, it is up to you to remove them from your life.

If you really want to experience absolute calmness, and communicate with your inner energy, try out Reiki and meditation. In this way, you will gradually unveil your defenses. You will look through the glass and see your reflection mirrored without any distortion. Get in contact with your energy centers and your chakras to reveal your power. Enhance your mental clarity, by removing the things that have been clouding your judgment. Find out the truth, and reach the depths of your spirituality. Relax and let go of the worries. Let go of anything that has been troubling you, preventing you from seeing what is out there for you.

You are most welcome to read my book *"Feminine Energy Awakening"* for an in-depth guide on how to awaken this raw force deep inside you. I will be very pleased to help you reach your higher self, embracing your divine nature. It is going to be a spectacular journey towards self-awareness. The world is your oyster, and there is so much you can do. Why should you settle for anything less than what you deserve in life?

❦ 4 ❧
WHY YOU MUST FIND YOUR DHARMA TO BECOME A MAGNET FOR ABUNDANCE

A re you eager to experience ecstasy and exultation in your life? Then you should find your dharma. There is no other way for you to reach genuine prosperity and feel blessed every single day of your life. We are spiritual beings first, after all. Our human manifestation is just a break from our eternal spirituality. First, let us start with an acknowledgment. Everyone has a special purpose in their life: this is the unique gift we have all been given and we are meant to share with the rest of the world.

Each of us has come to this world to discover their true self. Our talents need expression; otherwise, they would just go to waste. However, it is essential that we understand what it means to have a special talent. Think about your life. What are you good at? In fact, what can you say you excel at without thinking twice? Maybe you are great at singing, dancing, building homes, or cooking. Some people are great at creative activities, while others are more practical. No matter what it is that you perform awesome at, you need to stick with it for good.

Now, some might claim that your talent is your way to make money. This is your way to acquire fame and wealth in a materialistic world. Nevertheless, this could not be further from the truth. What you should focus on is helping others. Serving humanity is of paramount importance. This will in turn help you become perfectly aligned with the Law of Dharma. Instead of competing with others, and trying to appear as the best in your field, accept your true calling. Dedicate your life to doing something that will benefit the wider community. Are you a wonderful teacher? Then teach, and allow others to become enlightened through your teachings.

"How can I help the world? What can I offer the world? How can my unique gifts make the world a better, more fun, or more efficient place?" This is not just wishful thinking. Rather than theoretical discussion, this should become the core of your behavior. Rather than trying to overpower others, you need to put them in the spotlight. Your talent and your blessings are there to help. They have been given to you as a vessel to improve the world. Do not ignore this purpose of yours. Fulfill your destiny by bringing joy and happiness to humanity.

Once you get rid of your constant struggle to prevail, you will feel lighter than ever before. As soon as you stop monetizing everything, you will realize that you have been dragging yourself down all this time. Life is not a contest. The world is not filled with enemies— people who you need to stumble on—in order to move up the ladder. There is no point in undermining others, simply to put yourself on a pedestal. You will never reach greatness unless you unveil you prove to be selfless: putting the greater good before anything else.

In modern society, serving others might sound contradictory to what we have been taught ever since we were little. Competitiveness has been advertised as a true virtue, and those who have excelled in a field were seen as leaders. They reaped the fruits of their hard labor, always in comparison with the rest of the world. Still, by doing so, we cannot experience the true meaning of solidarity. We cannot understand how wonderful it feels to help others, without having in the back of our mind the possibility of gaining any benefit out of the process.

As soon as you strip yourself of the burdens that have been weighing you down, you will immediately change your mindset. You will start seeing things in a new perspective, and your entire world will change. No longer being a slave of your own desire and personal gains, you will be free to enjoy life as it really is. This is where the magic starts. The glory of the world unfolds before your eyes, and you start attracting abundance effortlessly. Sounds amazing, right? Try not to waste anymore time. Find your dharma and let life reveal its special purpose for you.

DO SOMETHING TO MANIFEST ABUNDANCE

Some people might think that good things come to those who are blessed. There are people who are lucky enough to receive many blessings in their life, and there really is no point in trying to claim the same on your own. If something comes your way, lucky you. If not, it was surely not meant to be. Well, although I did say that greatness comes effortlessly, this does not mean that you should just sit idle, doing nothing. On the contrary, you must be sure that you are on the right track. The best way to do that is to find your dharma. Comprehend your purpose in life, and concentrate on how to spark joy in another person's life. As simple as that!

What do you do in order to truly reach your deepest thoughts? What is it that drives you towards your higher self? It is essential that you clarify that prior to reassessing your priorities in life. Many people find it helpful to write a journal. Through scripting, you get to identify your weaknesses and reverse any negative situations. When you write something, you immediately make it appear more tangible. In this way, you cannot help but notice that. What you have written is now part of your reality. The scripting process allows you to spot the mistakes in their path, so as to avoid ever making them again. This is a great way to start, but it is not enough.

Meditation is another method used widely so that individuals reach their spiritual presence. You indulge in daily meditation sessions when you get in touch with your inner self. In this way, you calm down your senses, and you reach out to nothingness. This is very important, as it enables you to connect deeply with your source energy. However beneficial meditation can be, it does not work wonders. If you want to relax, it is a great tool to help you get rid of the tension, introducing you to utter calmness. Nevertheless, it takes more than that to attract abundance in your life. As I said before, you need to act. You need to do something, which will allow you to shift your life.

It is not enough to find your unique talent in life. Once you do find what it is, you should not ignore it. Why would you ever want to ignore your talent: your natural inclination in life? You have been given this gift in order to do something. If you just let it go to waste, then you might as well stop trying to improve your life altogether. On the contrary, you should channel your talent in a way that offers something to the rest of the world. If you are a great seamstress, then why not try using that to make amazing clothes for those in need? For those of you who are great at writing, how about you dedicate some time teaching creative writing? There are endless options out there just waiting for you to seize the moment.

When you find your talent, and you let it wither, you do not just cause damage to yourself. This would be self-destructive, but it would only concern you. You would be the one to blame for not following through your ambitions, your hopes, and dreams. However, the truth points out a different aspect as well. You also deprive the world of the opportunity to benefit from this very talent. Rather than contributing to humanity, you choose to sabotage your talent. You do not show others what you are made of, and you settle for less. This results in much fewer possibilities to shine. How can you expect to elevate your spirit and rejoice? A talent is meant to be shared for a greater purpose, so that it enables you to reach divinity.

A talent is a gift not only given to a specific individual, but to humanity as a whole. The world will only be balanced if everyone puts their talent to great use. Therefore, it is your duty to share your talent with the world. It is not up to you to decide, as you are not responsible for acquiring the talent in the first place. As soon as you wrap your mind around that concept, it will become clear what you have been destined to do all along. You will no longer have doubts as to whether you should pursue your dreams, or follow the path your intuition dictates. Just remember, practicing your talent must make you feel happy, satisfied, and complete.

I know that you might be baffled as to what you need to do. You may not know how to behave, in order to succeed in your path towards success. Even if you have the talent, how can you channel it in a meaningful way? What if you are uncertain as to your talent in the first place? Deepak Chopra has analyzed the seven spiritual laws which lead to successful living. These are the vessels which will bring you closer to your divine self. Below, you can read all about these laws that act as guidelines for you to follow. Be sure to structure your life in a way that allows you to respect and love others.

A Glimpse at the Seven Spiritual Laws of Success

In his book, *"The Seven Spiritual Laws of Success,"* Deepak Chopra M.D. reveals how to reach your divinity by finding your timeless spiritual nature. Unlike what you might think, there is no reason for you to strive nonstop, pushing yourself to the limits. When you observe nature, what do you see? A tree grows from a seed, without putting any real effort in the process. It is only natural, so it happens. In a similar pattern, you should let your spirit free, and enjoy watching yourself grow into the divine being you have always been intended to become.

There are seven spiritual laws, guiding you throughout your journey to achieve success. First of all, there is the *Law of Pure Potentiality*. This is a time for you to enjoy silence, ideally meditating once or twice per day. During this time, you sit still and embrace the lack of judgment. The world is filled with potential in their purest form. Moving on, the second law is the *Law of Giving*. This is an exceptional method for making others happy. Give them a gift: it does not have to be something expensive. Just a small gesture of how much you think of others. Even a compliment will do. When others give you a gift, or a compliment, accept with a big smile upon your face. Giving and receiving are two different sides of the very same coin.

The *Law of Karma* is next. Every action in your life generates an equal amount of energy. This energy is directed to you; if you wrong someone or cause pain, then this is going to target you right back. Therefore, you must make sure that you only bring happiness to the world. As a result, you will be showered with love and happiness yourself. Karma is a word often used in modern society, but it rarely has to do with something accurate. It is not a matter of revenge. No matter what it is you think Karma represents, it is just a reflection of the Law of Attraction.

The fourth law is the *Law of Least Effort*. According to that, you need to accept others exactly the way they are. Do not try to change them. Respectively, accept yourself and take responsibility for your actions. If you are constantly draining your own energy, simply to find out that others cling to their behavioral patterns no matter what, this harms you, not them. As soon as you wrap your mind around this, you will see that it is not your place to modify other people's behavior. What you need to focus on is how to accept them. Obviously, you need to accept yourself before accepting anyone else in your life.

The *Law of Intention and Desire* is another wonderful means to reach success. You should acknowledge that every desire comes with its fulfillment. This is an inherent procedure. In case you cannot fulfill a desire, you must understand that there is a reason behind that. Otherwise, you are bound to achieve what you desire in life. The universe will do its best to align, in order for you to get what you want. However, there are things that you should not receive in life. Once the universe picks up on that, it withholds this desire of yours.

Moving on, the sixth law is the *Law of Detachment*. It is important to allow others to be, without forcing them to comply with what you want. Everyone should be free to be whoever they feel like, without any restrictions applied by others. Even if you want someone into your life, you cannot force them. Always remember that life will play out exactly how it was meant to from the beginning of time. Detachment is very important when manifesting. Therefore, you should keep in mind that you cannot spend every moment clinging to your manifestations. You cannot waste your time, always thinking of what you desire. Instead, you need to let go, and watch the magic as it happens.

Last but definitely not least, there is the *Law of Dharma*. As mentioned above, this means discovering your higher self. This is the final destination, leading you exactly where you were meant to be. According to your unique talent in life, you are expected to use it to serve others. This is your deepest purpose in life, allowing you to reach new heights. Do not turn your back to solidarity and unconditional love towards humanity. Your spiritual greatness unfolds through this graceful purpose fulfillment. It is in your hands to discover ways in which you can use your unique talent for good. Remember that it will not only benefit the community, but it will also return to you as a bundle of positive energy (Chopra, 1994).

𝕏 5 𝕏

MANIFESTING LOVE

"All you need is love," at least according to The Beatles and their brilliant song. (Wikipedia Contributors, 2019) Everybody wants to love and feel loved in this world. It is such a wonderful sensation, making you feel warm inside. Along with love comes intimacy, respect, and companionship. Two individuals share their hopes and dreams. They share their fears and find shelter to one another. It is one of the most profound experiences in life. Many people claim that they have been lacking something crucial, until they found their partner. They even refer to that partner as their "better half," or their "significant other."

Each person is free to love whoever truly makes them happy. There are no taboos in love, no hidden agendas, no judgment standing in the way. Such a noble sentiment should not be smeared by negative thoughts or prejudice. Love is meant to take you to the moon, lifting your body and spirit. You no longer walk on the ground: you feel like flying. Who can stand in the way and pass judgment on who you want to share this splendid feeling with? It is a pure form of art, and there are no boundaries in art.

Love is a powerful driving force, motivating people to reach their greatness. People tend to become better once they have found someone who loves them. They put aside their selfishness, and they do things to benefit another human being. In other words, they serve humanity. Is that not what dharma is all about? As a result, they find a new purpose in their life, and it makes them better people. Even though they had been living on their own all this time, now they have discovered a new way of seeing things.

However, love is not so easy to experience. There are many people who have never found somebody to make them feel this way. At the same time, there are those who have never been loved...at least, not in the way they had been looking forward to being loved. Eluding love throughout your life seems extremely saddening. But, how can it be? Why is it that not everyone finds their perfect match? Is it really that difficult to run into the love of your life?

Ever since we are little, we get used to anticipating Prince Charming: he is going to come to our rescue. However, why would we want to let another person take charge of our life in the first place? There is no point in feeling helpless. Love does not have to be like that *"quid pro quo."* You should love someone because you want to, not because you have to do so. It is important to realize that you can survive without love. You are the one who will change your life and shape it exactly the way you have always wanted. Love will set you free and allow you to reach new heights. This is not a matter of survival; instead, it is the pursuit of happiness that defines one's need to love.

After having clarified that, it is necessary to appreciate the meaning of love manifestation. If you want to attract who you are going to love, you ought to figure out how to do so. Why waste your time surrounded by people who you do not find appealing? Why spend countless hours feeling sorry for yourself? Rather than settling for a loveless life, you need to take matters into your own hands, and call out love's name. You have the key to unlock the door and experience what you have been craving for your whole life. No one else is responsible to do that but you.

By manifesting love, you will have the opportunity to attract the feelings that you want others to show you. Remember all these endless nights when you have been visualizing the partner of your dreams? Now time has come to reincarnate those dreams. Instill life into your fantasies, and reach out to what you want to taste. The sweet agony of love, the memories that stay imprinted within your mind, the adrenaline spike, and the magic moments you spend together. Your heart skips a beat, and you feel like you have found your soulmate. Sounds breathtaking, right?

ATTRACT YOUR PERFECT MATE

Become a love magnet, and attract the partner of your dreams. In order to do so, you must project love. Otherwise, how can you receive it? It is a matter of balancing the energies. If you remain idle, avoiding to feel genuine emotions, and constantly struggling to build fences, then this is exactly what you are going to get in return.

One of the best ways for you to attract love is through EFT tapping. I have shown you earlier in the book how to change your body's vibration frequencies through this powerful technique. In this case, I am going to focus on the method of magnetizing the person you want, inviting them into your life. You can do that by indulging in a simple, yet very effective session. What you need to do is relax, and dedicate some time to tap specific meridian points of your body while at the same time repeating romantic affirmations. This will not only elevate the energy you are emitting, but it will also allow you to calm down your senses, and focus on what is important.

Try to get rid of any distractions. After all, you should dedicate these moments towards visualizing what you want to achieve, when it comes to feelings. "Why do you want to attract love?", "Are you worthy of being worshiped?", "What makes you a great person for someone to fall in love with?"; these are some of the questions you need to answer through this tapping experience. You must clarify all these issues before being able to move forward with attracting your dream partner.

Start slow by convincing yourself of what you should already know. "I love myself, and I honor myself. I am worthy of being loved, and I deserve to love someone deeply" is your opening line. This sets the tone of what comes next, which is none other than your love claims. You are an independent, powerful being that longs for sincere affection. You are not willing to settle for anything short of that, which should be non-negotiable. Since you have set the bar so high, it is only fair that you maintain absolute focus throughout the process.

Whatever insecurities you may have, now is the right time to encounter them. Change the way you feel about your alleged "flaws" through pointing out how invalid they are. For example, have you spent your whole life thinking that you are ugly and undeserving of love? This is what has dragged you down, preventing you from experiencing the true wonder of affection: you should change this conviction. Take a look at yourself. What is it that makes you smile? When you do smile, do you notice your eyes shining? It is true: you are beautiful. Add that to your affirmation.

Starting from the external part of your palms, as always, you must continue tapping at the face. The third eye area, right between your eyebrows, beneath your eyes, on your cheekbones, and above and below your mouth: these are all excellent parts stimulating energy. Then, move down a little. Tap your throat, which is where another important energy center is located. This is crucial for communicating your thoughts and your emotions. Next, you should tap above your chest, and reach your heart. Gently tap there, and feel your body aligning to your heartbeat. It is your circadian rhythm, so enjoy this perfect balance you have achieved.

End your EFT tapping session with a deep breath. I am sure you are feeling better, having boosted your confidence. Moreover, you must have increased your focus on what you need to pursue in life. Love is not something distant, and it is hardly out of your reach. However, you should reach out your hand and touch it. Even after having found love, you need to be delicate, and always strive to make your relationship stronger. There is no other secret to a healthy relationship other than brutal honesty, unconditional respect, and hard work.

Commitment in the Relationship

I am sure you are going to reach your goal and get the partner of your dreams, as long as you follow the guidelines that I have shared with you in this book. Nevertheless, this is just the beginning. First of all, allow me to congratulate you on having manifested the right person in your life. Now you need to become accustomed to the idea that this person is going to stay right by your side for as long as you want. There is no reason why you should not embrace the whole "till death do us part" thing, assuming that you like that idea. But, we should face it: there are still several bumps along the way threatening to destroy what you have already accomplished.

Keeping a relationship is just as hard as attracting it in the first place. You need to make sure that the relationship is always thriving through an ongoing process of evaluation. As you go, you need to check the status, and report any negative glitches. In this way, you can assess, and remedy everything ahead of time. I know this is easier said than done. Still, you must pay attention. Some people tend to let go, and settle for the fact that they have found a special individual in their life. They stop trying, which means they give up and never do anything to improve themselves.

If you are determined to maintain a viable relationship for the long run, then you must remember to water the flower of your love. This is the only way for you to ensure that it remains thoroughly flourished, and never dries out due to lack of care. I know you will be expected to do more than what you might have been used to, but it is definitely worth it. Since you have chosen a specific person to be your partner, you need to show respect and deep understanding. Do not just harvest the fruit of your labor. A relationship is a living and breathing organism. Unless it is nurtured, it is going to die out sooner or later.

Although each relationship has its ups and downs, one thing is for sure. You should keep the fire burning in order to maintain your initial passion. Remember what has drawn you to that person and what has made you fall in love with them. Why have you gone to extremes to conquer their heart? It is the same person standing before your eyes, asking to be loved eternally. Why have you stopped trying? There is nothing worse than indifference. I am sure you would hate it, drowning in a relationship that stagnates. Do not contribute to decay when you can instead breath fresh air to it.

Let your inspiration lead the way. Surprise your significant other, letting them know that you still care. It does not have to be something big. Just a flower or a morning note neatly placed by the bedside table. A text message you send on your way to work, expressing your true emotions. How about you get out of your comfort zone for a while? Even if you do not know how to cook, give it a try. Prepare a special dinner just for the two of you. Your partner is going to love that gesture. Even if the result is not up to par, it will mean something truly wonderful for your relationship. Then, celebrate your milestones. An anniversary is somewhat the norm, but try to figure out other things in your common path that have stood out among the rest. The first time you went on a vacation overseas, or the day you moved in together. These are small victories you should cherish for a lifetime.

Prepare yourself for some losing battles. Even if they seem that way, they allow both of you to let some steam off and move on with the good things about your relationship that have kept you going all this time. Compromising is not such a bad strategy by default, especially when the prize is your happiness. I am not saying that you should oppress your feelings, or give in to impossible demands. No, of course not. If that happens, then you have attracted the right person in your life. Reassess your priorities, think of what you actually want, and project that to the world.

Last but definitely not least, find the right balance between doing things together and allowing some space for your partner to breathe. It seems tricky, but you will get there. Just think of it as an opportunity to catch up with your friends, read, take on a new hobby, or just chill. There is no point in spending every single moment together with your partner: you will both feel suffocated in the end. Why subject your relationship to this ordeal? Instead, make every moment you spend together count. Do things that you will be looking forward to throughout the week. Your experience should be fun!

Now that you have cleared the air as to how to manifest love, how about attracting a specific person in your life? I am sure you have already set your mind on someone or you are pretty close to finding the ONE. What happens next?

MANIFESTING A SPECIFIC PERSON

I
t is amazing to acknowledge that you are ready to love and be loved back. This shows that you have matured in life and you want to share your emotional treasures with someone special. But, who is this person? We are often open to meeting new people, inviting them into our lives, and evaluating our relationship as we go. However, there are times when we have already decided about who we would like to see in our life. Even though at first this might sound very restrictive, in time you will realize that it is a true blessing in disguise. Not only do we know how we want to feel, but we are also certain about who we want to feel it with. How awesome is that?

There are moments in life when the universe seems to be fully aligned with your desires. In these moments, you feel like the luckiest person alive. Falling in love definitely ranks high in that list. Especially when your love interest shows exactly the same emotions, you are over the moon! How could you not be? I am well aware of how intoxicating love can be, overwhelming you with that warm sensation that lets you know you have found your perfect match. Yet, not everyone gets to be that lucky. Unfortunately, on several occasions you will encounter people who have never found their match; on the contrary, there are those who have found them, but they have been left craving for a relationship.

I know what you are about to say. You cannot force somebody to have feelings for you...or can you? Let me rephrase that for you, in order to reflect reality. Instead of worrying about forcing another person to have feelings for you, how about you admit that they would be lucky to have you in their life? You are not a random person, are you? In that sense, you are doing them a favor. You are opening their eyes, attracting them into a life filled with light, happiness, and abundance. This should be your mentality, prior to engaging in a sensational love hunt.

The most important thing to remember is that your body's vibration frequency needs to be balanced with theirs. In order to do that, you must be extremely careful. No negative thoughts should flood your mind, as they will most likely lead to a low frequency. Unless you wish to settle for a life in misery, and disappointment, avoid such thoughts for good. You need to open yourself to positive emotions, gradually building your momentum. What a better way to achieve that than through a wonderful visualization? Allow me to show you how to invite this special someone into your life. Of course, you can indulge in this session even when you do not have a specific person in mind.

Visualize the person you want to see in your life, and picture every little detail. The color of their hair, the sparkle in their eyes, the small lines on their face, the shape of their body, the way they dress, and the way they make their hair. These are all special touches which have led you to love them so dearly in the first place. Hence, they deserve to be mentioned, and you need to focus on these special attributes of your love interest. Once you have painted their picture in your mind, you are ready to move forward to the next step. Feel them moving towards you, getting closer and closer with every breath you take.

As soon as your dream partner has reached right before your eyes, and you can feel their breath warming your lips, you can concentrate on their movements. Feel their hands slowly touching your palms, arms, and shoulders. They are moving upwards, and then they are touching your neck, and finally your face. Feel their fingers fondling your cheeks and then touching your hair. They are smiling at you, and they are whispering in your ears. I am sure this gives you goosebumps, and you are already experiencing that exciting sensation.

Now, remember that you must combine this visualization along with several positive personal affirmations. In this way, you will optimize the effect of this session on your mindset, and eventually on the energy you emit. Below, I have prepared some of my favorite affirmations to share with you:

- I love myself deeply and unconditionally.
- I am worthy of being loved.
- My chosen partner and I share deep, true feelings of love and devotion.
- I am happy to have my significant other into my life.
- My chosen partner is 100% committed to our relationship.
- Our relationship is true, meaningful, and honest.
- We are both happy to be in this relationship that will last for a lifetime.
- My significant other respects me totally and honors my personality.
- I am grateful for all the love I receive in this world.
- I am thankful about all the blessings I have in life.
- My chosen partner is deeply in love with me, and the feeling is mutual.
- I am sure that our relationship is going to last forever.
- There is nothing that can separate me from my significant other.
- I have been blessed with love; I have been showered with love.
- My chosen partner and I are a wonderful couple.
- My significant other and I are meant to be together.
- I am so happy to have such a loving, caring partner in my life.
- I have no doubt that me and my partner belong together.
- My chosen partner always tells me how beautiful and intelligent I am.

- I have a deep spiritual, physical, and emotional connection with my partner.

By repeating those affirmations, you will strengthen your self-confidence. In this way, you will project it to the world, attracting what you deserve. The specific person you have set your mind on will have no other option, but to fall into your arms. This will happen sooner or later, there is no need for you to worry about that. Just embrace your destiny, prepare for what is about to take place, and wait for the magic to unfold before your eyes.

HOW TO GET YOUR EX BACK

Dealing with an ex can be really heartbreaking, I am well aware of that. I am sure there are deep wounds that never seem to heal, no matter how far you have moved on in your life. There is always a person who has scarred you, and this scar has become part of who you are. In case your ex is a toxic person, I am going to insist on letting go and seeking a new partner. Although you may feel hooked on this individual, you should know that you need to pursue light in your life; avoid the darkness and all the toxicity that lurks in the shadows. It will drag you down, drain you of your energy, and leave you exhausted, disappointed, and helpless. Is this the life you have been dreaming of throughout this manifesting process?

Let us assume that your ex is not toxic. Take a moment and concentrate on what has driven you away from each other. Was it an act of infidelity? If this is the case, then what will stop your partner from doing the same thing again in the future? Maybe you have just drifted apart due to lack of common interests. Distance can get in the way and mess with relationships. Not many people can handle endless miles separating them day-by-day. Perhaps that flame has burned out eventually, leaving you reminiscing those times when you could not get enough of each other.

No matter what the special circumstances have been that lead to your breakup, you need to do some serious soul searching. What you need to figure out is if you truly want to have your ex coming back to you. Do you honestly want to get your ex back, or is it just a whim? You do not care to admit it, but your separation might have caused you the repulsed desire to get your partner back in your life. On some occasions, people tend to forget about the bad things. They focus on the wonderful memories that they share with their ex, often idolizing them. So, take a deep breath: ask yourself if this is really what you want to achieve through manifesting.

Even after having concluded that you want to try again with your ex, you still have to come to terms with a disturbing fact. No matter what has happened between you two, you were the one to blame. Of course, this does not mean that you should beat yourself up or assume full responsibility. It is important, however, that you know where to look, and connect the dots. When the relationship collapsed, you may have tried hard to understand why. Perhaps you confronted your ex in order to find out the truth. Yet, you need to realize what has been the driving force that resulted in pure havoc. What has led to your relationship collapsing right before your very eyes? Is it still a mystery to you?

I know that it has been a while since you two were a couple. Nevertheless, it would be great if you could recall some memories you have of the time period prior to your breakup. If you look more closely, you will start noticing a pattern. You had started questioning your partner's feelings. In fact, you had begun thinking that you were not enough. You had lived in fear of abandonment, practically waiting for your partner to break up with you. Maybe you had read the signs wrong, or maybe there was a slight sliver of evidence backing your fears. Either way, your thoughts had been piling up for so long, creating low body's vibration frequencies.

As a consequence, you basically attracted the breakup. You made sure that your partner started seeing these signs, feeling them deep inside, and eventually leaving you. Does that sound familiar? Is this the way you behaved before you broke up with your ex? I am pretty sure about the answer, as this is how quantum physics works. You think about something intensely, ignoring anything else. Over time, your thoughts become the reality. You project them to the world and end up attracting the very same thing. You have been looking forward to using this specific mechanism in your favor, manifesting love, wealth, and happiness.

Every experience can turn into a lesson for you, allowing you to become wiser as time passes by. Never again should you project these negative thoughts to the universe, as they are bound to come back and sabotage your life. You do not need to worry about a potential breakup. If you do break up, then this is what you were always meant to do in your journey towards reaching your higher self. *"Que sera, sera"*, or else *"Whatever will be, will be."* (*Que sera*, 2019) No one knows what the future holds for them, but you should have faith in your divine spirit.

Assuming that you still want to get your ex back, you need to start projecting that to the world. Begin visualizing that you already have your ex in your life. Close your eyes, and think of your partner's presence beside you. They are standing right in front of you, almost touching you. Take a moment and observe every single detail about their physical appearance, as well as their posture. Are they showing any affection towards you? I bet they are. It is prudent to enhance this visualization with some positive affirmations. Feel their arms around you, and their breath as they are whispering sweet nothings. Imagine that you are already together, just like I have shown you above, targeting a specific person.

Repeat the same ritual as often as you like, always maintaining the same positive attitude. Your ex will be drawn to you sooner or later, enabling you to enjoy your relationship with them. Do not be pessimistic: believe deep in your soul that you are together. This is the first and most important step to take in order for this dream of yours to come true. Just remember that some things work out exactly the way they are supposed to, even if we do not want to admit that. That being said, set out on this wonderful adventure and pursue your fantasies!

A Common Mistake to Avoid Like the Plague

You have mastered the art of manifesting a specific person, and you are ready to put theory into practice. Are you starting to feel excited? Be careful, though, as you may fall for the oldest trick in the book and sabotage your own endeavor. Have you ever felt like nothing ever works out the way you have expected it to, despite your hard labor? Well, there is a reason why this happens. Although you have planned out every single detail, it seems that you have neglected the importance of a little thing. It is a pity to let that stand in the way, and prevent you from reaching your "happy ending."

Let us get more specific about the single worst scenario that can play out when manifesting love. You focus on the way your partner is going to be. While doing so, you concentrate on their physical appearance, and then you outline the features you want them to have. A kind and gentle partner, witty, understanding, with a great sense of humor, and wealth: seems like a keeper, right? Next, you manifest the feelings you expect of this partner. This specific person must be madly in love with you, showering you with affection. What a better way to boost your self-confidence than a constant reminder that you are unique?

I am sure you are reading these lines with a huge smile on your face. I do not blame you: this is what we all want in life! It is so invigorating to experience love in its purest form, making you feel like a million dollars. Nevertheless, what about the other way around? Have you ever thought about that? It is awesome to find a person who truly loves. A person who will go above and beyond just to be with you. It is what we all dream, a partner who will be utterly devoted to us no matter what. This is what most of us have grown up to wish for, when we lay in bed at night. Still, how about our feelings towards them? Do they not matter as well?

The huge mistake that you are about to make is not to pay attention to the way you feel towards your manifested love interest. How will you feel towards your special person? Unless you manifest that too, you risk ending up with an unfulfilled romance. This means that you will enjoy the love, and affection of the person you have attracted in your life. However, your feelings will not be mutual. You will not be madly in love with your dream partner, and this will spoil your long anticipated emotional equilibrium. In the end, you will feel like you are to blame for all this mess. After all, the relationship is never going to last, if you do not share the same enthusiasm. Sooner or later, it will crumble into dust.

Do not get me wrong: it is perfectly understandable to love yourself, and make sure that you attract someone who loves you the way you deserve to be loved. You should continue pursuing happiness and sparking the feelings you are entitled to in life. At the same time, though, you must make room for manifesting how you want to feel towards your dream partner. It goes without even saying that you should aim at a balanced relationship, meaning you feel pretty much what your significant other feels. Otherwise, your chances of staying together for a long time decrease dramatically.

In a nutshell, the big drawback you need to steer clear from is the lack of focus on who the partner is going to be and how you are feeling about the specific individual. If you are determined to embody the experience of mutual, intense love, you need to be careful throughout your manifestation. Whether you are thinking of a specific person who already exists in your life, or you are manifesting a totally new individual, you must pay attention to your feelings towards them. Incorporate how you are going to feel, so you avoid the realization that you are just not that into the person you have invited in your life, because let me tell you, this is going to be a hot mess!

❧ 7 ❧

THE POWERFUL MANIFESTING
TECHNIQUES

There are so many wonderful things just waiting ahead in your life, I can promise you that. The thing is that every single person has different desires, different needs, and different wants. How can you manifest these things into your life? This book aims at giving you all the necessary tools which will allow you to welcome anything you have been dreaming of into your life. Manifestation is real and it is out there. It is now in your hand to reach out and grab exactly what you like.

In this chapter, I am going to focus on journaling and scripting. These are the two sides of the same coin, meant to serve as your lucky charm. I know some of you might be skeptical as to why you need to devote time and write down what you want to achieve in your life. *"Isn't visualization enough?"* you may argue. Writing is a cathartic activity, which can help you cleanse out your body from within, just like a detoxification diet would. Even though you are having doubts, let me reassure you that you are going to love it.

First of all, you need to create a lovely atmosphere. You must be looking forward to your scripting time. This should not be a boring, tedious concept. It should not be something you only do because you have to. If you consider journaling a mere obligation, then it is only going to backfire. You will never receive what you are writing about, which will definitely lead to more doubts on your behalf. This is a vicious cycle that benefits no one. I would strongly advise you to give it a chance, and dive right into scripting with a positive attitude.

Find a journal that truly makes your heart beat faster. It needs to be something you enjoy writing in. You do not have to go overboard when it comes to the actual cost of the journal. Just pick something that appeals to you a lot. Maybe add some color, or find a luxurious treat that you can resort to for manifesting your dreams. Alternatively, you can also write letters on a piece of paper. Literally the sky's the limit, and you can experiment with scented paper, fancy pens, and pencils. Of course, you can always resort to the digital form of journaling. Yet, nothing beats the sensation of writing on a piece of paper. You watch letters transformed into words, and this is something you made from scratch. It is such a creative activity.

THERE IS NO RIGHT OR WRONG AS TO WHERE YOU SHOULD WRITE. Some people sit on their desk, whereas others prefer to be fully relaxed, so they choose their bed or a comfortable sofa. Just do whatever makes your boat float, because you need to feel good about the entire process; otherwise, you will not stick to this habit for long. Create a cozy ambiance, maybe put on some lounge music that relaxes you. Light a scented candle with a lovely aromatic character, and sip on your favorite herbal tea. Get those creative juices flowing. This is your moment, so relish it.

Now that you know how to write, it is equally important to clarify what you should write about in your journal. Some people think that they should write everything they have ever wished for, exactly like they did back in the day with their letters to Santa Claus. As a result, they end up completing a list of things they want to attract in their life, and then they expect for every wish to come true just like that. However, scripting does not work in this way. This can only work when you are a child, provided that your parents take a moment and read through your list. Then, you can expect to find a great surprise under the Christmas tree.

Start slow, and be consistent. Do not just try out scripting when you have nothing better to do. Instead, you should make sure to indulge in this relaxing activity on a daily basis. This will allow you to become fully conscious of the things you want to attract in your life. When you begin this creative habit, you will soon find yourself drawn by your emotions. An inner drive will guide your actions, and enable you to fill whole pages with your thoughts, your projections, your intentions, and positive affirmations.

SCRIPTING AS A GREAT LAW OF ATTRACTION FORCE

Scripting will most likely change your life, as long as you let it. In order to do so, you need to decode its purpose. When you are journaling, you are writing about the things that you want to draw into your life. This is the very core of the Law of Attraction, after all. Vibration attracts vibration. First of all, you should be very excited about the things that you write. Do not just go through the motions, without adding emotion into the mix. If you avoid feeling when you write, then you might as well stop right now.

Besides, look at it this way. When are you used to acting, rather than contemplating? I am sure feelings are involved in your actions. They grow, and flood you with an energy that wants to burst out of your body. This is when you act and release that energy. Do not just write indifferently. Make every word count. If you are not in the mood, do something else. You can always write when you feel like it. In this way, your vibration will skyrocket, and you can attract the things you write about effortlessly. If you are emotionally involved, I guarantee that your manifestation will become a lot more intense.

That being said, there is a widespread misconception that you had better steer clear from when scripting. You might get overly enthusiastic, and wish for things that are never going to happen. For example, you cannot project to the universe your desire to get a lot taller. This can never happen, no matter how hard you try. In other words, you should believe in what you are scripting, setting fairly realistic goals that you can achieve. Do not get me wrong: you can always dream big, but you need to include things that you believe can happen in scripting. In a different situation, your subconscious brain decodes your desire as false, and does nothing to proceed with its realization.

When you write in your journal, remember to be precise. You need to have mental clarity, and include details about what you want to achieve. If you only mention your goal, then how can you expect it to be realized within a specific time period? In avoidance of any distortion of your desire, leave no room for speculation. Do not be vague; instead, add as many little things as you can into your description. Some people might be afraid of offering too much information. This could backfire, since it would limit their options, right? I do not know if you share this opinion, but the Law of Attraction does not work like that.

I am telling you again, do not shy away from details. For instance, when you are manifesting a specific person, you should include their physical appearance. Along with that, you should add the personality traits that you love about them, as much as those that you want to avoid. Finally, you need to be accurate in your time frame. When did you meet this person and where? What do you both feel? All these details will help you accomplish your goals exactly in the way you want. Otherwise, it will be pretty much like you are gambling. Obviously, it is possible that you do not have your mind set on a particular person. You do not need to, as long as you describe the specific characteristics you have been searching for in that person.

A lot of people tend to be indecisive in their scripting experiences. They start manifesting one idea, and after a few days they move onto the next. It is a rollercoaster of emotions, as one manifestation is constantly swiped with another one. This can result in pure havoc and chaos. You are looking for balance, not chaotic situations. When you do not follow through with your description, you cannot make it happen. If you are afraid of making a decision, then you should not write about anything in life. In fact, you should not engage in the Law of Attraction. But, is it not the main purpose of reading this book? Make a decision, and wear it with pride. Commit to your decision and enjoy it as it becomes reality.

One word of caution before moving forward with an outline of what to include in your scripting: do not fall for the *"wishful writing"* trap. As mentioned before, you should have the attitude of already witnessing the benefits of your accomplishments in life. Do not write as if you are wishing for something to become true. This would confuse the universe, and it would certainly create a different vibration for you. It is already true, and you are experiencing its wonders to the fullest. You are projecting how you feel, after accomplishing that particular thing, and keeping it into your life. As a result, you attract the very same emotions. As simple as that!

A Template That Makes Scripting a Piece of Cake

There really is no "one-size-fits-all" approach in scripting. You basically start writing in your journal, and you watch the magic happen. In fact, before you know it, you will see your thoughts transformed into words. They will literally flow from your mind and fill the blank sheets of paper with your most wonderful wishes for the future. It is purely great to channel these dreams and fantasies of yours into something creative. After a while, you can turn to these journals and read all about them. This is a way to keep track of your progress, evaluating how much you have actually managed to manifest into your life. Pen and paper is all you need in order to form the foundations for reaching your goals. Indulge in freewriting, so as to let your thoughts lead the way.

Confidence building scripting is a great way to boost your ego and truly appreciate yourself. Even if at first you will feel slightly uncomfortable, you do need to adhere to the routine of praising yourself for everything you have accomplished so far. This is not a race, so it does not matter how much time it takes you to achieve your milestones. The only thing that matters is that you move towards the right direction. A technique used to build confidence, and project what you want to attract, is through writing letters.

In case you want to write a letter of gratitude, a thank you letter, or a note that explains what you have succeeded in doing, I have prepared a practical template to use. In this way, you no longer have to worry about what to write. Just follow the guidelines below, copy, and add to your manifesting routine. It is best that you complete writing the letter, and then keep it somewhere within your reach. Read it out loud, so that you get to believe every single word you are saying. You can keep it by your bedside table, and read it when you wake up, and again when you go to sleep. Do so for 20 to 30 days, and then store it somewhere neatly. When you come across that letter after some time, you will be greatly surprised!

Thank you, _____ (This is where you insert the name this letter is addressed to. It can be what you believe in, a guardian angel, a spirit, a mythical presence, a person you look up to, an influencer, or a specific person in your life.)

I am truly grateful for everything I have in my life. It is great to have such health, happiness, love, and abundance showering my existence. (In this section, you start by giving thanks for all the good things that have happened in your life and all these things that you want to achieve. In that way, you mention as if you were already experiencing them.)

I have achieved my personal, and professional goals _____ (This is the time to be specific, so write down everything you want to have in your life: both as a person and as a professional.)

I now have _____ I have been enjoying love, and happiness every single day.

Thank you, thank you, thank you so much _____ (Repeat the name you have addressed this letter to.)

As you can see, this is a quite simple, yet effective outline for a gratitude letter. You can always add your personal touches, of course. By all means, be creative. Still, do not be modest, or shy away from claiming what you want to achieve. Be firm and positive. Write like you are already reaping the fruit of your manifestation. Activate the feeling of already having these things in your life. Then allow yourself to forget what you have written. Move on: concentrate on other things. Clear your thoughts, be creative, and live your life. Last but not least, be pleasantly surprised as these things come into your life.

Use this template to create a gratitude letter directed to your parents, or the people who have inspired you in your journey so far. Make sure to write thank you letters, big or small, to those who have contributed to who you are. Apart from that, do not forget to write down letters including gratitude to people who you would want to have in your life. Write as if they have already helped you and you want to give thanks to them. In this way, you cultivate the feeling of gratitude on various levels. You enhance the feelings you have experienced in life, and at the same time, you are projecting the emotions you want to experience.

❧ 8 ❧

MANIFESTING YOUR DESIRE IN
30 DAYS

D o you want your desire to come into fruition? Very well. How much time can you invest in accomplishing that goal? Time is money, and you should not let it go to waste. Instead, you need to make every minute count towards your self-accomplishment. Luckily for you, there is no rule stating that you should spend an enormous amount of time preparing for the Law of Attraction. It is all about you coming into alignment with what you want. Once you find that precious balance, the world is your oyster.

Strengthen what you believe of yourself. This is one of the primary goals you should set. Journal every day and describe whatever you do. In this way, you will be able to understand where you are blocking your success. On the other hand, journaling will also enable you to identify all the situations where you have showered yourself with positive energy. The things that are showing up in your life derive from your vibrations. Unless you realize that, you can never expect to reach these goals of yours.

Believe in your inner power, as it is indisputable. Positive affirmations will help you in your effort to grasp your power. Get in the frequency of your desire. Believe that you are worthy of amazing things in life. You should not let anyone tell you differently. You are great, and this is non-negotiable. What makes you unique, though? Think about that and write down as your thoughts become reality. What you must make sure of is that you project that confidence to the world. This will in turn open up a whole new world of opportunities, because this is what you will draw closer to you.

If you are determined to succeed, then it is essential that you share your initial enthusiasm about the whole process of manifesting. Why did you look this philosophy up in the first place? I am sure that you have read somewhere about this wonderful secret that makes your mindset shift. From your experience in life, this is exactly what has been dragging you down, so you thought you would give it a try. A few minutes later, you were blown away by the innumerable possibilities unfolded before your eyes.

What has changed since your first reaction? The Law of Attraction is a powerful gift, so why would you ever get disappointed? If you are seeing no tangible results, maybe you should reevaluate your strategies. Assuming you want to speed up the process, there are a lot of things that you can do. Powerful manifestations that I am describing below will allow you to achieve what you want in a fraction of the time it would normally require for your manifestation to complete. Take charge of your life, and start working towards making things happen.

Do the things that make you feel better. In this way, you will lift your spirit and ensure that your body's vibration frequency becomes radically elevated. Make the Law of Attraction fun again. Avoid suppressing your desires, and succumbing to what society dictates. Now it is your time to shine. Enjoy the ride, and do not settle for any other substitute. Get inspired, since it is the inspiration that drives your spirit to greatness. Be mindful of the experience, and appreciate the moment. This is what being in the present means, after all.

Finally, I would have to insist on stating what you want. Of course, scripting is a wonderful way to manifest your desires. However, you should never underestimate the power of expressing those desires verbally. You can do it out loud, or you can simply whisper these projections. Do not worry—the universe is always listening. The fact that you say all the things that you want to receive in life will only speed the procedure up, allowing you to enjoy the benefits of having your wishes realized. Listening to your own voice repeating those desires is quite soothing and also enables you to believe in them completely.

Having said all that, and right before moving on to the powerful manifestations that will speed up the entire process of attracting what you want in life, take a moment to contemplate the following verse: "*As you set out for Ithaca, hope the voyage is a long one, full of adventure and full of discovery*", as the great Greek poet Constantine P. Cavafy has said (Marlene, 2018). Sometimes, the journey is more important than the destination itself.

MANIFESTING WITH THE MOON PHASES

A spectacular way for you to fulfill your desires in a small time period is to manifest with the moon phases. As you may know, the moon has the ability to control water. We mainly consist of water, which is why we feel so strongly connected to the moon itself. Many people report that they feel influenced by the full moon, and their behavior changes dramatically. It is true that the moon's energy is at its highest peak during the full moon, which is why it takes its toll on everyone on Earth. Besides, a new moon represents a new beginning. A whole new journey starts all over again. This is a clean slate, without blockages in your energy.

In order for you to manifest using the moon phases, you need to write down your wish as it has already happened. As you are well aware of, this is called "living in the present." Unlike projecting a wish to the future, you should make it clear that your wish has been fulfilled. After completing the letter, you should write down the date. This will allow you to be conscious of your desire. You are not vague in wishing for something to happen. Apart from setting a time frame, you also need to be detailed as to how it made you feel. Be very particular, and describe everything. As a consequence, you will enjoy the benefits of exactly what it is that you have wanted to attract in your life.

Visualization is the key to success in manifesting. So, as soon as you have finished writing the letter, you are encouraged to follow a ritual. Bury this piece of paper into the ground. You can choose to bury it in your garden or perhaps in your balcony. Although it might seem strange, placing the paper in the soil will help you stimulate the visualization. It will complete the whole picture, and you will be envisioning that this piece of paper is a seed. This is what connects you to your desire. Let that seed grow and turn into the satisfaction of your desire.

In two weeks, the full moon will take place. Some people will see their wish come true during the full moon. These are the lucky ones! If you are not one of them, do not worry: you just need to write down another letter. This letter will be all about yourself. You will concentrate on your virtues, and write down all the amazing affirmations that describe who you really are. Include things like *"I am loveable," "I am amazing," "My heart is pure gold," "I deserve to be loved," "I deserve to be cherished and respected."* Then, use the very same ritual: bury this piece of paper. Alternatively, you can throw it in the garbage or even flush it down the toilet. But, let us face it, burying it is the best stimulation for your representation of a growing seed.

Waning gibbous is when the moon starts fading away, after the full moon. This is the time for a third letter. In this letter, you will get rid of all the negative emotions you might be experiencing. This time, you will use affirmations, such as *"I release anxiety,"* and *"I release worry,"* so all these self limiting beliefs are gone. Self-limiting affirmations serve a great purpose. They help you change your negative thoughts and prevent any blockage. Unlike the two previous papers, you should burn this one. In this way, you visualize the release of this negative energy. Get rid of it symbolically.

As the moon takes its different shapes, and a full cycle is complete, your desire will soon come true. You can use the energies of the universe in your favor. Achieve the absolute balance with your divine feminine energy, and benefit from this powerful gift you have been given in life. Let nothing hold you back, and make no excuses. You deserve to reach your goals without wasting any more time.

How to Manifest With Water

Have you ever heard of Dr. Masaru Emoto? He was a scientist and became worldwide famous for his water experiments. What he did was place water of the very same source into different jars and then write down different words on these jars. Some words had a positive meaning, such as love or affection. Others were negative emotions, just like hate or disappointment. Afterwards, Dr. Emoto froze the water and observed the jars. What he saw was amazing. The jars containing water and "positive words" had created crystals of immense beauty and symmetry. On the other hand, jars with "negative words" had abnormal-shaped crystals, without any beauty or balance (Pitkanen, 2018). Water holds the vibration of words or anything attached to it.

As mentioned a little earlier in the manifestation using the moon phases, people are mostly made of water. This means that our body gets affected by the moon, as the moon controls water. At the same time, Emoto's experiment has proven that our body is also affected by the vibration of words. Can you fully grasp how huge this realization is? If you are determined to manifest your desire into a month or less, then water manifestation is a great way to do that. You will only need a tall, glass bottle with a cap, a piece of paper, and something to write on it.

On a new moon, it is the best time for you to start this powerful manifestation. However, you can do that whenever you want. Just keep in mind that the new moon reflects new beginnings. You first need to take the paper, and write positive affirmations about your desire. For instance, do you want to get a promotion? Then, start writing about how you feel about having already got that promotion. Remember that you must always write "in the present" and not project your future desires.

What you should be careful of is the particular choice of words you use while journaling. I know that this is oddly specific, but you need to pay attention to the slightest things if you want to be successful in your manifestation. Do not use any word that has been charged with a negative vibe. Rather than saying "*I am not a failure,*" you can try saying "*I am successful, I thrive in what I do.*" Even though both sentences have pretty much the same meaning, the first sentence is negatively charged.

Write down your feelings in detail, and be very specific. Take the time to think of all the aspects that are relevant to this promotion. How much money are you going to get? What opportunities will come up eventually? What special perks does this promotion have for you? Before wrapping up the scripting process, be thankful for this desire that you have achieved. Then, get that bottle. Fill it with water, and hold it with both your hands. Have that letter by your side, and start reading each sentence out loud.

As soon as you finish reading each sentence, close your eyes. Repeat the same affirmation over and over again. Do that until you believe that the specific affirmation is true. In this way, you will be transferring your positive vibration to the water bottle. When you are done with one sentence, move on to the next. Once you have finished with the letter, take a sip of the water. As you might have guessed, this water will be charged with the positive vibrations of your entire letter. What a healing potion this is, right?

This sip will remind your body of your desire, and charge it with the positive vibration of your affirmations. Then, place the bottle where it can be charged with the great energy of the new moon. It will absorb this energy, and you can sip on the water for the next month or so. Every time you drink a little water, your body will be energized with this powerful, positive feeling. Do this consistently, and you will fulfill this desire of yours before you know it!

9

15 DAILY MANIFESTING HABITS
TO SHAPE YOUR OUTER REALITY

It is important to spend your days productively, in a way that enhances your manifesting process. This will allow you to optimize your performance, and attract even more wonderful things into your life. I am sure that you are already on the right track, focusing on how to project into the world all the blessings you want to receive. With the help you get from this book, I am positive that you are going to triumph. However, this does not mean that you should neglect all the other aspects of your life. In fact, there are several habits you can incorporate into your daily routine, in order to lift your spirit and guide you to a new, improved way of living.

Make sure that you commit to this new lifestyle, experimenting with the habits that I have gathered below for you. Even though some of them might appear a little strict, do give them a chance. You will be amazed at the results, since you will shape your outer reality exactly the way you have always hoped for in your dreams. Nothing should hold you back from experiencing the new you: feeling happier, healthier, more accomplished, and wealthier than ever before.

1. Write down notes with your goals, and review them frequently. This is one of the top habits you should

incorporate into your life. Write about everything you want to achieve, and include the date. These can be short-term goals, or life-changing targets. It does not matter if they are important. What matters is that you evaluate your journey, trying to figure out how to make things better for you in the long run. You can use an app in order to keep track more conveniently.

2. Memorize those goals. Of course, I am not saying that you should memorize the entire journal you keep, although that would be impressive! However, you need to repeat the most important goals of yours until you learn them by heart. Then, you will have the opportunity to repeat the goals in your mind again and again. Especially before sleep, it is a great habit to tell yourself all those affirmations that you would like to manifest into your life.

3. Break down the goals you have, and celebrate milestones. It is only fair to break down your goals into smaller ones. For instance, if you want to lose 50 pounds, you cannot have just one goal. Instead, focus on the first milestone of losing 5% of your initial weight. When you do, celebrate it! Reward yourself for your dedication. This will only strengthen your motivation and allow you to continue.

4. Scripting. I have already referred to the power of scripting, or keeping a journal, but I cannot stress that enough. Make it a habit to write down on a daily basis, because it definitely helps you channel your energy. It also allows you to stick to your goals, as it helps you to steer clear of all the temptations to stall. You do not need any delays, do you?

5. Use a vision board. Even if you do not like this in the first place, I assure you that you will be hooked. You know how important visualization can be for manifesting your desires. Use images on a board, where you interpret these desires and shape them into reality. The board can either be of physical form, or digital. Rather than closing your eyes and envisioning those things, open them and enjoy!

6. Listen to meditations or audiobooks, before going to sleep.

There are so many amazing audiobooks out there. Yet, most people are drowned in a hectic lifestyle, with literally no time to dedicate to themselves. Enjoy the productivity, and just relax right before bedtime. All this knowledge will be infused in your mind without you even realizing it.

7. Cultivate a feeling of abundance and practice gratitude. When you feel abundant, you project it to the world, and it comes back to you. This is the concept you want to adhere to when cultivating that feeling of abundance. At the same time, it is equally crucial to practice gratitude. Be thankful for all your blessings, and let the universe know.

8. Smile. As simple as that!

9. Be kind to yourself. Why would you ever want to beat yourself up for something you did? You should cherish who you are, and love yourself beyond limitations.

10. Practice diaphragmatic breathing. Try breathing deeply from your belly. This enables you to use your parasympathetic nervous system, which helps digestion and promotes relaxation.

11. Quit watching TV or at least keep it to a minimum. The time you spend in front of the TV goes to waste. You avoid thinking, and your brain gets overwhelmed by easily digested information and content of no meaning whatsoever. In addition, TV prevents you from indulging in much more beneficial activities; as you know, time is money.

12. Work out regularly. When you work out, you immediately elevate your body's vibration frequency. This alone should motivate you to incorporate a workout routine into your lifestyle. Plus, when you exercise, you release endorphins and feel happy. Your health will be grateful, too!

13. Eat healthy. Your body is a vessel, and you need to treat it with respect. Sometimes we neglect its value, only focusing on our mental clarity and spiritual presence. Choose a viable diet, which not only nourishes your body but also helps it heal. Vegetarianism in all its versions, veganism, paleo diet, or the Mediterranean diet: these are all great options for

you to experiment with, always with respect to seasonality and local produce.

14. Connect with nature. It is a magnificent privilege to go out in nature and truly align with its grandeur. Go out for a walk, taking in the fresh air while listening to the birds chirping. Smell the aromas of the blossomed flowers, look at the chromatic combinations in the fields, or up in the sky. Enjoy a lovely sunrise or a captivating sunset. There are so many things that will bring balance between you, and your surroundings.

15. Wake up early in the morning. Last but not least, you should at least try to be an early bird. When you wake up early, you have more time to devote to things that will improve your quality of life. Have a long shower, meditate, or prepare a healthy breakfast. Give yourself the time you need to wake up smoothly, awaken your senses with a sip of your favorite beverage, and prepare your mind and body for a day filled with energy.

That is it! Of course, you are most welcome to add more positive habits that contribute to the advancement of your manifestation experience. Focus on what makes you feel good deep inside, since this is what you are going to emit. In return, happiness attracts happiness. Joy sparks joy and returns in multitude. Love, affection, affluence, success, or growth: you name it!

RELEASE RESISTANCE WHEN EXPECTING MANIFESTATIONS

You have started this wonderful journey towards reaching your higher self and manifesting your desires into the world. During this journey, you have been through some truly groundbreaking changes in your life. You have learned how to relax and avoid negative thoughts. In addition, you have mastered the art of manifesting a specific emotion or a particular person. You have been through the ups and downs of this amazing experience, and now you are ready to enjoy the benefits of manifestation in all its glory.

However, there is a fear growing deep inside you. Although it has begun as a tiny sliver of doubt, it has now gone out of proportion. All these expectations that you have when it comes to manifesting might sound natural to you. Nonetheless, they can transform from motivational patterns into the cause of your frustration. Does that seem contradictory? Well, there is a fine line here and this is what I want to discuss. Expectations are typically strong beliefs that you have about something, which you are certain is going to happen. For example, one of your expectations can be to become abundant in life. You are sure it is on its way, and this makes you feel awesome.

A specific time passes by, and you have not reached the point where you feel abundance flowing into your life. Even though the expectations of wealth gave you joy in the past, it is now starting to threaten you. More than that, you are beginning to question the effectiveness of your behavior. *"Am I doing this the right way?"*, *"Why is manifesting not working for me?"*, *"What is wrong with me?"*, and *"How long do I still have to wait until I get what I deserve in life?"* These are just a few of the questions that might be crawling into your mind, causing you extreme discomfort.

If your expectations are causing you frustration, then they build up resistance. Therefore, you need to release that. It is hurting you, while at the same time blocking your progress towards fulfilling your goals. I know that I may have touched a chord with this description, but it is best to deal with it as soon as it occurs. Rather than settling for a constant feeling of stress, you need to relax. You need to release the tension, which is caused by resistance. What you ought to do is switch your mindset to hope. Do not worry about how you can achieve that. It is quite simple, yet truly effective as a strategy.

Expecting something to happen means that you are counting backwards until it does happen. This might trigger anticipation beyond the point you can handle. As a result, it brings you anxiety and eventually leads to disappointment. You cannot spend your days concerned as to why your desire has not manifested yet. This is counterproductive, and offers no real benefit to you. On the other hand, you can reverse the situation pretty easily. What you do is concentrate on the feeling of expectation, hoping for your desire to manifest promptly. Does that sound hard?

This shift in your mindset will reflect on your daily affirmations, too. You will no longer think of the following: "*I expect my desire to manifest. Why hasn't it already manifested? I must be doing something wrong.*" Instead, you will have more positive thoughts: "*I hope that my desire manifests. I hope that I am doing everything right, and my desire manifests soon.*" Although these two attitudes bear some resemblance, the truth is that they are very different. The first one adds stress in the mix, whereas the second soothes your soul, filling you with a positive vibe.

Practice Makes Perfect

It would be spectacular to change your life from one moment to the next. Unfortunately, this is not how life works. Where would the fun be in that? If you were able to transform your life so easily, it would not feel that great to accomplish one of your goals. It would be just a mere part of reality, something that would happen either way. "*No pain, no gain*" as I am sure you have heard numerous times before. Nevertheless, this does not mean that you should not try to improve your existence and attract everything you want to receive.

This is what the Law of Attraction does, giving you a helping hand to reach the goals that you have set for yourself. It goes without even saying that you cannot expect to fulfill these goals overnight. Take for instance the list I have shared with you containing 15 daily manifestation habits that will work wonders for you. This is great, and you should definitely start ticking those habits. Yet, can you do all of these things? Are you sure? Even if you can, how long do you think it will take you?

Start slow, and work yourself up the ladder, adding more into the mix when you feel more comfortable. In this case, you can start by smiling more every day and following a healthy diet. You can also engage in physical activity by walking to and from the office. Buy a journal, and start documenting your days. Figure out the positive affirmations that work for you, so as to memorize and repeat on a daily basis. Cut down on the time you spend in front of the TV, and instead go out and admire nature.

Gradually build your life in the way that makes you happier and more satisfied. Take comfort as you realize how much you have grown, realizing exactly what matters in life, and putting all the toxic thoughts aside. Even if you fall off the wagon, never beat yourself up over this. Regard it as a small obstacle, which will only make you stronger. Do not consider it the tip of the iceberg, since this will bring you a great deal of stress for the future.

Consistency is vital in this endeavor. You will need to commit to your efforts, and follow your habits for the long run. Otherwise, all your hard labor will go to waste. By being consistent, you increase your chances of success. Remember that you want to change the vibration frequency of your body. The best way to do so is by emitting positive energy from within, and you can only succeed in that through long-term changes in the way you feel. Stick to this regime, and watch the benefits as they present themselves to you.

10

MANIFESTATION SKYROCKETING
MEDITATIONS

A re you ready for some powerful, calming, and upbeat guided manifesting for women meditations? In this section of the book, I am going to show you exactly how you can meditate, in order to attract the specific things you want in your life. These meditations will show you how to focus on what is most important to you. They are outlined in detail for your optimal convenience. I have made sure to include step-by-step meditations that cover everything you need so that you can record the text from the book and listen back to it as a guided meditation if you want. How about it?

Remember that you need to focus on a single goal every time you manifest. If you get super excited—and include multiple wishes in your manifestation—then you are about to experience some serious disappointment. The truth is that the manifestation gets split many ways if you have more than one desire added in the mix. As a result, the energy you emit will not draw the results that you are anticipating. To avoid all that discomfort, it is best to concentrate on a single goal. In this way, you will be able to achieve that faster, and far more efficiently.

MEDITATION TO MANIFEST ANYTHING

As the title suggests, this is a flexible meditation that can be used pretty much for anything you wish to attract.

Take a deep breath. This is the time to clear your mind of every other thought. Let go of the physical world. Just focus on the thing you want to attract in your life. Manifesting can be relevant to anything in life. However, you need to be extra specific.

Do not be afraid of specifying exactly what it is that you want to manifest. Is it to earn $20,000 by the end of the month? Or is it to get your ex back within the next 10 days? Maybe your wish is to get healthier and lower your cholesterol levels as soon as possible. Do you want to attract a successful associate to join your business by the end of this term? Think of every single detail, and avoid being vague.

Breathe deeply again, feeling absolutely relaxed. As you are relaxing, you can access your deeper spirit more easily. You open up, and believe in this meditation. Remember that you are already experiencing what you want to manifest. Believe in that, as you are taking another deep breath.

You are now feeling your body letting go of every single muscle. Your muscles become loose and they are falling down beneath you, starting from your legs. Your belly is relaxed, and the tension on your neck escapes you. You relax your jaw and these muscles around your eyes. Your whole body experiences that calmness and lightness in your life.

Take another deep breath, and try to notice any negative feeling. I am sure that there are still persistent emotions that prevent you from reaching out to your divine feminine energy. Let go of every negative feeling, like fear, doubt, or depression. Replace these feelings with positive energy flowing through your entire body.

Now, concentrate on what you want to manifest. How would you feel if you already had that in your life? How would this affect your life? Would it also change the lives of those around you? Imagine all the consequences of this manifestation.

Take a moment to visualize how you introduce that to those within your circle of family and friends. Imagine their reactions, and visualize your discussions with them. You are already seeing it unfold before your eyes.

Envision your life as you are enjoying this manifestation in your life. Sense it: feel it in your core. See your life now after having attracted this desire in your life, and focus on the feelings you experience. Are you happy? Does this make you feel more motivated? This is already happening in the present—there is no doubt about it.

You have no restrictions, so it does not make any difference how this manifestation came to be. It is thanks to your limitless possibilities that you have attracted it into your life, and now you are enjoying all the benefits surrounding it. You have what you want right now, and this is all that matters. This is your reality; this is your moment to shine.

Continue with your visualization. You can see it right before your eyes, so you know it is there. If it is not physical, you are seeing the reactions of that desire manifested in your life, so there is no doubt for you that it has happened.

Now let it go: let all these positive feelings and visualizations go. Do not worry: you are not going to lose your manifestation. This will allow you to take action and manifest this desire in your life for good. Every decision you make will bring you closer to your goal.

Take a deep breath and relax. You know that your subconscious will guide you, so that you effortlessly receive what you want. This is your belief—no one can take it away from you. Breathe deeply and return back to reality, knowing that your manifestation is on its way.

Shifting Your Reality

If you want to attract great things in life, you need to change your frequency. This is a wonderful meditation which will help you shift your vibration, and in turn allow you to manifest everything in your life.

This is a powerful meditation that will transform your life and your entire physical presence. Get comfortable: laying down somewhere cozy.

Take three deep breaths, inhaling through the nose and exhaling through mouth. This will help you relax, soothe your senses completely, and prepare to shift your frequencies.

Imagine your thoughts and the tension of your day slowly fading away, so that you are light and calm. Then, visualize an abundant light. Start relaxing your feet and your ankles, going up to your thighs and your belly.

Move upwards, allowing every cell in your body to absorb the wonderful light that you are visualizing. Continue all the way up to your chest, your neck, and now your face. The light is shining on your beautiful face and now above your head.

Now, visualize two pairs of shoes. The ones on the left reflect your old self. They are worn out, and they look unappealing. The shoes on the right represent your new self, so you want to walk on these new shoes.

Imagine that you are walking towards your manifestation. Your desire has already come true, so you are enjoying this walk on your new shoes, feeling wonderful. How does this make you feel? Experience this entire process in detail.

What does this manifestation feel like? What changes have taken place? See them vividly. Expand on this feeling even more. Allow this warm feeling envelope itself through your body. How do you feel?

You have already received your manifestation. Observe the reactions of those around you, and interpret your own behavior. Allow yourself to soak in this experience, as you are enjoying every single aspect of this manifestation in your life. What other opportunities does this bring?

See the changes on the new you, as you are growing more mature, more intelligent, and more accomplished. You are living your dream. You are the best version of yourself. All your desires are taking place before your eyes, and you are feeling great. You are feeling complete.

Take a last deep breath, and remember your new you. Get used to this feeling, as this is going to attract everything you want in your life. Repeat the same meditation as often as you like, at least daily for a whole month. Open your eyes, stretch a little, and smile.

MEDITATION TO MANIFEST A LOVING RELATIONSHIP

If you want to attract love into your life, then you should follow this powerful meditation. It will help you open up and get ready to connect to the world.

Take a deep breath, and make sure that you are in the moment. Lift your chest so that your lungs expand. Fill your lungs with fresh air as much as you can. Hold that air for a little while, and breathe out gently. Repeat the same thing twice.

Surrender your body weight to the surface underneath you, and feel yourself becoming lighter. Feel your energy flow gently. Breath effortlessly, and visualize two roses side-by-side. Notice the colors of these roses and the texture of their petals.

See these roses clearly, keeping your eyes closed. Take one of these two roses, and keep it in the palm of your hand. Offer it as a gift to your heart. Be kind and gentle. Watch it fill the space within your heart. It has blossomed, opening up to your chest.

This is a reminder of the fact you need to love yourself. Admire this rose of deep love. It represents who you are, along with your tenderness, your honesty, and your ability to connect deeply with those around you. It shows that you can connect even with those who you have not met yet.

Think of the warmth of your smile and the softness of your touch. You are unique, with innate goodness showering those around you. Remind yourself, if you do not already know, that you are a true blessing to this world.

Now go ahead, and visualize the second rose. Observe it carefully, looking at each little detail. It is delicate and fresh. If you look closer, you will realize the second rose is unique, too. This will bring a loving, caring partner in your life.

Feel your desire to love and be loved: you are worthy of experiencing this feeling. Congratulate yourself on your courage for loving and supporting yourself. You should be happy, because you want to show affection to another person.

You are enjoying a unique bond with your partner, and this is your honest intention. See the two roses merging at the center of your heart. This connection has been accomplished. The two flowers commit to loving yourself fully, while also welcoming the love of your partner. It is a wonderful feeling deriving from your pure intention.

The universe is guiding you always, leading you towards a person who nurtures you, loves you, respects you, and accepts who you really are. A person who cherishes every moment they spend with you, and loves you unconditionally.

Visualize the two roses again: repeat the same meditation every time you wish to attract love into your life. Breathe deeply again, and concentrate on your body. Feel your body becoming grounded again, and softly open your eyes.

Meditation to Attract Success in Life

This is a great meditation which will welcome success into your life. It is mainly used to attract wealth and business accomplishments.

You must keep your body grounded, so you need to find a position where you sit comfortably. Your feet are on the ground, and your shoulders are relaxed, looking down. Breathe deeply and slowly.

Take a moment and bring thoughts of success to mind. Visualize that, indulging in the greatest expressions of success. Your mind can dive right in the most glorious moments of success, and bring them before your eyes.

You should be proud of what you have accomplished so far, given these moments of success that come to mind. Now is the time for you to take full control of your life, enhancing success.

This is the time to start doing all the things that you have been postponing. No more struggles, no more anxiety, and no more stress as you are letting go of your past habits and incorporating new ones into your life. You are ready to take the next step toward success. You are ready for positive habits, such as getting more organized.

In the past, you have procrastinated. Putting off projects, avoiding work, and making bad choices is no longer an option. Now, you are ready to create the foundation for a positive life.

Take a deep breath, and expand your chest. Breathe deeply and slowly again. You have realized that you must take care of some unpleasant things and tackle them with mastery. This is the only way for you to succeed in your adult life. Do not avoid the tasks that you did not favor in the past.

Do not let your ego take control, as you are ready to get into the path of success. Get rid of all the negative thoughts and projections. This will allow the positive energy to flow through your body and into your daily life.

What are the habits that you want to incorporate into your life? Visualize them in detail, so as to experience them and make a difference in your success journey. Do you want to commit to waking up early or tackling the accounting of your business? Turn these thoughts into habits.

You are ready to experience a sense of freedom as you grow stronger emotionally, and mentally. This is the path towards success for you. Everyday the work becomes easier to accomplish, and you thrive pursuing new positive habits.

Make a pledge that you will adhere to your new commitments, no matter how difficult they might be. This is the way to reach greatness, so you are determined to succeed. Your success will come naturally, freely, and effortlessly.

Breathe deeply again, and slowly regain consciousness of your body. You have remained grounded, so open your eyes, and welcome your new reality. Welcome to the path of success.

✵ II ✵

MANIFESTING ROAD BLOCKS AND
HOW TO CRUSH THEM

"*Why is the Law of Attraction not working for me?*"—This is probably the most frequently asked question and paints a picture I feel the need to explain further. It is true that not all people who practice the Law of Attraction see results. Or to be more precise, they do not see them unless they realize what they have been doing wrong. If you want to be successful in this path to attracting all the things you want in your life, you need to study. It is essential that you fully comprehend the science behind the Law of Attraction.

I have explained the basic principles of the Law of Attraction earlier in my book. Basically, you need to understand that vibration attracts vibration, and every person has their own resonant frequency. When you reach that resonant frequency, you can literally succeed in anything. What you ought to do is to change your vibrational frequency and your thought patterns so that you align yourself to what you want. Universe works with time and space. Therefore, you need to constantly align to that vibrational frequency. Otherwise, you will not be able to attract it into your life.

That being said, we are only human. This means that we are bound to make mistakes. A negative thought, a period of feeling under the weather, or a panic attack: these can cause blockages and hinder your progress while trying to manifest your wishes. It is only fair that you realize what these obstacles really are in order to deal with them efficiently. How do you know what your blockages are; how can you get rid of these blockages in your way to manifest your desires into the world?

You attract more of what you feel, rather than what you think of at a time. The universe will pick up on why you want something in your life. If you are manifesting something because of a certain lack, the universe will disprove you, and you will end up without getting what you want. This is why it is crucial that you feel abundance, so as to attract affluence right back at you. Try to feel the fulfillment. Your emotions and your thoughts are the ones that are shaping your reality: it is not the other way around.

Trying to make something happen is very masculine, and this is great on several occasions. However, this does not work well in your love life—think of it that way. When you are trying to visualize your dream partner, you should focus on allowing them to come into your life. This is where you would like to shift to your feminine energy. Otherwise, you would be starting from a position of lack. You want to manifest your dream partner, because you do not have them. This is going to be catastrophic for you. When it comes to matters of the heart, you ought to bring out your feminine energy. This will help you set the tone for welcoming what you already visualize into your life.

Another blockage that you may not even think of is the impact of your manifestations to others. Although you would think they do not really affect your manifestation, they actually do. Imagine that you want to travel the world and discover different cultures. This is a marvelous opportunity for you, filling you with excitement and joy. How about your overprotective parents, though, or your loving partner? Do they share your enthusiasm, or is this manifestation going to bring out negative emotions?

What you need to do in this case is to reinterpret the negative consequences of your manifested desire into empowering beliefs. You should make sure that your manifestation sparks joy on everyone else, which is how the universe will grant you your wish. For example, you can visualize that you communicate with your parents frequently, and that they are proud of you for pursuing your goals. Maybe you struggle with that reinterpretation at first. This will only get better over time, since your brain will gradually be rewired into thinking positively. Not only that, but your subconscious brain will follow the same path.

Changing your mind too often will prevent you from manifesting what you want. This happens because you want so many different things, and you do not allow yourself enough time to process and align to that particular vibrational frequency to attract it. Do not just move on, but instead find what you actually want. Stick to that goal, and do not let go until it has indeed manifested. Then you can of course pursue something different. However, do not confuse the universe like that, and do not lose focus.

Before completing this reference of road blocks that you might encounter during manifesting, you should clarify the difference between meditation and focused visualization. Unless you realize how to use either of these techniques, you may block your progress when manifesting. So, through meditation, you use mindfulness to gain awareness. You basically shift your mindset, trying to reach mental clarity and a calm state of mind. On the other hand, focused visualization allows you to focus on what you want to attract. It is more straightforward and can be done anytime. You simply get rid of distractions, and concentrate on the one thing you want to achieve.

DOES YOUR PERSONAL INTEGRITY GET IN THE WAY?

In or out of integrity? You cannot fake the Law of Attraction.

Integrity is your set of principles: your moral code that drives you to behave in a specific way. Every single time you do something that is not in alignment with your core values, you feel negative vibrations. This in turn leads to obstacles in your path towards manifesting your desires into reality. Does that sound like something you want in your life? This is a rhetorical question, since I know how devoted you are towards manifesting and reaching your higher self.

There is an antidote, which can be used to counteract this particular poison. Be honest, pay your debts, and avoid borrowing things from others. Be kind to people around you, and never gossip about them. Never make a promise that you do not intend to keep. Be punctual and fair in your decisions. Everything you say and do should be guided by these values. Do not fall into the vortex of telling lies, even if you consider them "white lies" or innocent. Even these lies will keep you from achieving your goals. The pure positive energy that you want into your life will be hindered.

It is important that you are true to yourself. Otherwise, you will be facing a moral dilemma. Even if you try to rationalize, you can never justify your actions by bending the truth. Just visualize that you are in the other person's shoes, the person you have been affecting with your behavior. How would you feel if something similar happened to you? If there was a person who behaved in a similar manner to you, would you be content? Or would you feel frustrated and out of place?

We all make mistakes, and this is pretty understandable. You cannot always be in control of your every thought, and you can expect to be tempted once every now and then. The world is a challenging place, after all. Every day, you interact with people. You make decisions about everything, from the smallest thing to the most important milestone. Remember that you are not in a contest: this is your life you are trying to optimize. After having slipped through a slippery slope of lies and dishonesty, you are going to make your life a lot more difficult.

What you need to commit to is personal accountability. When you always make up excuses about behaving badly, you do that to feel better with your particular choices. Yet, this does not work well in the long run. After a while, you will notice the change in your frequency vibration. Your entire balance will be crushed, leaving you hanging.

Even if you are doing everything else right, you will not get to see the results that you have anticipated through your manifesting journey.

Redeem yourself by doing your best to maintain the balance in the world. You cannot change your past—this is non-negotiable. However, through redeeming, you will change your vibration while doing something nice to another person; this will allow your vibration to shift. It is a constant struggle, and you must be aware of the hardships. However, you should never behave in a way that harms others. This is the epitome of dropping your vibration and damaging your psyche. How can you anticipate to manifest after that?

Five Harmful Myths About Manifesting That Might Be Hurting You

It makes sense that you dig deeper into the Law of Attraction and the concept of manifesting your desires into the world. There is a plethora of information out there, so it is very easy for you to reach out and gather a multitude of resources to study. However, you should take everything with a grain of salt. In other words, do not just fall for every single video you watch on YouTube.

Do not believe in everything you hear, especially if that contradicts your existing beliefs or your knowledge on the matter. Believe me, sometimes less is more. Below, I am going to refer to five of the most dangerous myths out there about manifesting. The reason I am doing it is to protect you, and motivate you to cross-check everything you learn about the Law of Attraction.

One of my personal favorites is the myth of "If/then." There are people claiming that you can manifest every single desire and get it with no questions asked. The only requirement is that you put the "If/then" rule into effect. This holds a deeper fear, though: I am talking about the exoneration trap. Life is filled with challenges. In order to achieve something, people need to dedicate time and effort. Dissatisfaction and not having the things we want is a part of our lives. Sometimes, when something you want does not manifest into your life, then this is a lesson from the universe. You should not think of it as a punishment. Being disappointed over having to struggle for something is counterproductive and totally distorts you from appreciating the true meaning of life.

Moving on, there is the misconception that you can manifest things, even when you are not ready to receive them in your life. This could not be further from the truth, though. You need to become the right person, in order to get the right things. Let me give you an example. If someone gets a million dollars, without having worked a single day in their life, then they are clueless as to how to invest that money. They have not gone through the process of earning the money, learning how to form a fruitful business, and so on. As a result, they basically live on borrowed time, and end up being broke. What is the point of receiving a blessing when you are clearly not ready to receive it at the specific time?

Another myth that might get in the way, and potentially harm you in your effort to manifest your desire into your life, is oversharing. I know that you are overly enthusiastic about the Law of Attraction. This is amazing, and I would like nothing more than to see your expectations met and even exceeded along the way. However, there is a thin line you should never cross. When you tell others what you are attempting to do, you are risking the possibility of attracting negative emotions. If they are jealous of your manifested success and happiness, they will project that negative energy to you. Are you sure you want that in your life?

You do not need to become secretive. Just filter the things you share, so as to maintain a balanced social life without any glitches along the way. I am not saying that you should become an introvert, or lie to people. In fact, I have explained how lies can have a negative effect on your manifestations. Nevertheless, there is no reason why others should know the slightest detail about how you have accomplished so much. Obviously, they do not have to know how much money you have in the bank and how the Law of Attraction has helped you in that. This can save you from a lot of pain: trust me.

The fourth myth about the Law of Attraction is definitely the fraction of time it takes in order to achieve your goals. Tell me honestly: how can you expect to bring something so wonderful into your life overnight? The claims are literally preposterous. It is exactly like claiming that a specific diet is going to help you lose 30 pounds in a single week. These claims cannot be validated, of course, and they mess with your determination. Once you see that you do not fulfill these manifestations in a short amount of time, it makes sense to get discouraged. Disbelief creeps in your mind and prevents your growth.

Finally, a myth that is constantly repeating itself about manifesting is the obsession over materialistic possessions. Many people think that getting money or a fancy house, will automatically erase any negative emotions they have. I wish things were that simple! Under no circumstances should you idolize money or possessions. They should not be your objective rather than a means to achieve what you want. The only thing that they can provide is peace of mind as to your financial future. They enable you to do more, but it is up to you how to handle the resources you receive.

As you can see, there are several misconceptions that can actually hinder you from your opportunity to shine and reach your personal goals. Set rational targets, and always evaluate the things that you read about or listen to in a podcast, a video, or a conversation. Have faith in your own power, and do whatever makes you happy without messing with your body's vibrational frequency. Now let us move forward to the final chapter of this book, where I lay out an inspiring daily ritual to help you manifest.

THE 30-MINUTE FEMININE MANIFESTATION DAILY RITUAL SECRET FORMULA

I t is important that you follow a daily ritual, which will allow you to start your day productively, feeling amazing. This is how to set the tone for your high vibrational frequency in order to attract what it is you want to manifest in your life. Of course, you can add your personal touches and make the perfect morning ritual to adhere to every single day. Wake up early in the morning, as this will allow you to appreciate nature at its finest moment. It is calm outside, as the world has not started its frenzy. You wake up and get ready for a full day of excitement. Making your bed will give you a sense of accomplishment, and this is a wonderful feeling to hold on to throughout the day. Write your own routine and stick it on your wall for inspiration: it works!

As soon as you wake up, you should open your curtains, and let that natural light bathe the room. This is a symbolic way to cleanse and purify the environment you are in, while at the same time lifting your spirit up high. Open the windows, and take in a deep breath of fresh air. That feels rejuvenating, right? Of course, it is all a matter of where you live. If you are in the countryside, or if you have a garden, you will smell the blossomed flowers and even listen to the birds chirping happily. Even if you are not, though, it does not matter. Appreciate where you are, and be in the moment.

Keep your home clean and decluttered. I cannot stress that enough. Your personal space is a reflection of what goes on inside you, which means that a cluttered home means you are a mess. How can you stand this chaotic situation? On the other hand, if you clean up on a regular basis, everything will be neatly stored. This will allow you to feel better, projecting it to the world around you. In a similar pattern, pay attention to your personal hygiene and the way you look. It has nothing to do with vanity. However, you should cherish yourself and treat you like the goddess you really are.

Now is the time to move on to the actual morning ritual, which will offer you the opportunity to expand your manifestation. It will not take more than 30 minutes, which is absolutely great. This is adequate time for you to dedicate to yourself, promoting your self-growth and ensuring that you are on the right track towards happiness, abundance, and love.

1. After waking up, you should take some time to focus on your breathing. This is a great way to calm your mind down and restore that perfect balance in your body. Breathe through the nose, and exhale through the mouth. Instead of the hectic breathing you have been accustomed to, try abdominal breathing. As a result, you will feel your lungs filled with air in their maximum capacity. Release the air back into the atmosphere gently. Now, cover one of your

nostrils and breathe through the other one. Even if you do not know this, we always use a single nostril to breathe in and out. This nostril shifts after a few hours. So controlling your breathing like that enables you to relax even further. You calm the mind, set your intention, trust in the uniyerse, and allow things to flow into our lives

2. Then, it is time to be thankful. Dedicate just five minutes for a gratitude meditation. Keep a gratitude journal, where you express your gratitude for all the blessings that you already have in your life. Use "as/if" sentences, in order to enhance this feeling of self-accomplishment. Close your eyes, and think about all the things you are grateful for in your life. You are healthy, you have a roof over your head, and you are surrounded by loving family and friends. It can be anything, as long as you feel grateful. Along with what you have already accomplished in life, you should also include the things you want to attract. These are things you need to draw closer to you, so make sure that you give thanks about already having them. This will create the perfect frequency, so that you can attract them promptly towards you. Do not forget to smile, as this is basically the manifestation of your happiness.

3. Devote some time to write daily in a journal, practicing your scripting. This is where you need to include your personal affirmations, which will boost your confidence and keep you motivated. Read through the affirmations that you have already written down, and leave the journal somewhere you can access very easily. Take some moments to repeat these affirmations out loud. When you do, you will immediately feel your spirit lift. You want that in your life. Obviously, you can practice scripting throughout the day, or even right before going to sleep. Nevertheless, early in the morning this activity will give you the energy boost you need for the day.

4. After having focused on your mental tasks, it is time to

remove the stagnant energy. You need to get active. I would
suggest engaging in a yoga session or pilates; however, it is
totally up to you. If you feel like it, you can dance to the
beat of your favorite music. Alternatively, you can stretch
and do some cardio. Getting on your treadmill is a great way
to feel the energy flow through your body while increasing
your vibrational frequency. It goes without even saying that
activities outdoors are even better. If the weather is fine, go
out for a walk or a jog.

5. Next, head to the bathroom. It is your time to relax and
wash away all the negative thoughts that have been running
through your mind. Take a shower, feeling the healing
properties of the water. Enjoy the relaxing atmosphere, as
you are soothing your muscles and awakening your senses
fully. Then, apply your makeup. Do whatever makes you feel
beautiful as you truly are. Be radiant with a glow that starts
from within, as you present yourself as your best version.
Finally, do not forget to smile! Pick the clothes you are
going to wear and get ready.

6. Last but not least, prepare a healthy breakfast. Start your
day eating wholesome foods, without any process. You can
have a smoothie, or a fruit salad. Be sure to include
superfoods, which allow you to get your omega-3s,
antioxidants, and vitamins for the day. Chia seeds, flaxseed,
avocado, or berries: these are all excellent foods to start
your day with, along with some herbal tea or coffee. This is
where you can relax and maybe go through your emails, or
scroll through your social media accounts. Listen to some
music, and make plans for the rest of your day.

Now you are perfectly aligned to the energy of the universe,
looking forward to attracting all the things you want to receive in your
life. Good morning, sunshine!

SAVE TIME BY MAKING ONE SMALL CHANGE IN YOUR MANIFESTING ROUTINE

What you want is to amplify your positive energy and empower your manifestation. rather than spending endless hours trying to make things work, you need to focus on what enhances your efforts. There are several things that you can do so as to minimize the time it takes for your manifesting routine to get into motion. You can use scented candles when meditating, or you may indulge in the power of herbs. However, if I had to pick just one thing to optimize your manifesting routine, that would be the use of crystals.

When crystals are used in your manifestation, they will boost your energy beyond compare. Although everything in the universe has its own vibration, there are items such as crystals that hold a much more powerful vibration. Therefore, they have the potential to amplify your intentions and project them to the world. This is what you want to achieve. Get the best results, dedicating the least time possible to receive them. Below, I have handpicked three crystals that are my favorite. All of them are perfect to use in your manifestations, as long as you respect their special characteristics.

Amethyst is an extraordinary crystal, which allows you to connect deeply to the source energy. You want that when you are trying to manifest your desires. Amethyst is a wonderful option, because it boosts your inner confidence and also soothes your senses. Amethyst is responsible for promoting your spiritual enlightenment, as it is aligned with the third eye chakra. By using amethyst in your manifestations, you purify the negativism around you, and you protect your energy preservation.

Rose quartz is another crystal that will help you when manifesting love, as it is called "the love stone" for a reason. This crystal is aligned with your heart chakra. If you have gone through a traumatic experience, rose quartz will empower your healing. When you are in a relationship, it makes sense that you use the rose quartz. This special crystal will enable you to attract compassion, love, and affection, bringing down the walls some people build in their heart. These are the attributes of a perfect relationship, right? If you do not have a relationship just yet, try placing the rose quartz underneath your bed and see what happens.

Finally, perhaps the best crystal to use to optimize your manifesting journey is citrine. Not only does it increase optimism, but it is also great for mental clarity and abundance. You would want a crystal that removes toxins: in a world where we are surrounded by toxic thoughts and people, this is of paramount importance. Remove all this negativism, and set your mind out for success. Now, in order for you to step into your personal power and build your confidence even more, you should use citrine. This crystal is connected to your solar plexus, which strengthens your intuition.

Obviously, you can experiment with many different crystals. There are wonderful precious items out there, including black obsidian, pyrite, green aventurine, and green jade. Moreover, you can go for the yellow sapphire, topaz, zircon, ruby, and hematite, just to name a few. As long as you read through the crystal's properties, you will be able to use them to your advantage. If you cannot decide, then you can mix them up together. In fact, some crystals work extremely well in combination.

Apart from buying these crystals, you need to know how to use them. First and foremost, you should cleanse the crystal thoroughly. You do not know where the crystal has been and who it has been used by. You should cleanse it out of any negative, stagnant energy. You can do that by taking it out in nature, possibly washing it in the crystalline waters of a small stream. This will also absorb the energy and life of nature. Of course, you can also clean it using running water at home. In addition, you can use Himalayan salt.

Next step is for you to charge the crystal you have just bought. Place it out under the moonlight, ideally during full moon. Be careful not to leave the crystal out in the sun, as its color will fade away. This applies to all crystals, not only citrine. Last, you need to consecrate on the crystal; in other words, you need to set your intentions. To do that properly, you must be well aware of the crystal's properties. Now you are ready to connect with the crystal on a deeper level. Hold it in your hands and bring it closer to your solar plexus. Close your eyes, maintaining high vibrations and a clear, pure mind. This is when you are expected to focus on what you want to manifest. Let your crystal know about it.

Nighttime Ritual

Have you ever considered sleep as a super long meditation session? Sleep enables your body to reset and get ready for another day filled with possibilities. Sometimes, people are so exhausted that they get in bed and fall asleep instantly. A minute has passed, maybe even less, and they are out—sleeping like babies. However, others experience trouble sleeping due to stress and too many thoughts flooding their brain. We need to face it: sleep is too long to endure negative energy.

This is why you need to take some time and engage in a simple, yet soothing nighttime ritual. You will feel lighter, and you will focus on what actually matters. There is no point in losing sleep, worrying about things that you cannot control. On the contrary, you can use sleep as a means to manifest. How about it? When sleeping, you get in direct contact with your subconscious brain. So, if you can channel your desires in a way that allows them to reach your subconscious, then you will be successful in your manifestation. It is definitely worth giving this a try. I promise you, it will change the way you feel and manifest!

First of all, prepare a soothing hot beverage. A cup of tea, like chamomile, will allow you to calm down. If you want, you can warm some milk. Do some stretching, and relax your muscles. Your body needs to feel free and light. By stretching, you release any tension from the body. This will prevent cramps or any other discomforting feelings that may disturb your sleep. Then, listen to a motivational podcast or a video filled with positive stuff that you can use as a source of inspiration. A guided meditation will get you primed and relax you deeply.

Clear out all the thoughts you have and all the stumbles that you may have encountered through the day. I am sure you have a lot on your plate but try to compartmentalize. Right before bedtime, you do not need to worry over things that you have no control over: this does not get you anywhere. It will only mess with your tranquility and most likely lead to a sleepless night. What you ought to do is amplify positive emotions, so as to shower yourself with them. They will guide you towards scripting. Talk yourself off the emotional ledge you have found yourself on, to help you find relief. Practice gratitude, as it naturally shifts us into a positive vibrational frequency. All that creates a positive wave of momentum in your life.

Of course, you should steer clear of technology before bed. Although swiping on your mobile phone might seem tempting, this will fill your mind with information to manifest. At least one hour before sleeping, lock these devices away and out of your reach. If you need extra motivation to do that, think of how the blue light emitted from these devices takes its toll on your body. It decreases the rate of producing melatonin, which is responsible for regulating sleep through controlling your circadian rhythm. Why would you deliberately mess with that?

Another thing you need to consider before sleeping is to meditate. It does not have to be sophisticated, or take up a lot of your precious time. You purely practice your breathing, so as to relax and eventually reach nothingness. Witness your senses, without any dialogue. Feel the breath, take in the smell, and listen to the sound of silence. This is the secret that will allow you to meditate properly. After having completed your meditation, you can now move forward with your focused visualization. As I mentioned earlier in the book, meditation enables you to maintain your calmness. Visualization, on the other hand, helps you focus on the one desire you want to manifest.

Finally, let go. Stop thinking. As you already know, the Law of Attraction does not work with expectations. Instead of attaching yourself to something, you need to detach. So, after having set your phones aside, after having listened to an inspirational video while sipping on jasmine tea or after having meditated and visualized your desires, now it is time to let go. Repeat the following lines, and stop thinking about anything: *"Universe, I am grateful for everything in my life. What will be, will be."*

AFTERWORD

I am so happy to see that you have completed reading my book on manifesting for women. I am so proud of you for reaching into your spiritual self and doing your best to improve your life on so many different levels. You deserve to be happy; therefore, you need to put theory into practice, and set out on this wonderful journey of the senses. Hopefully, this has been an eye-opening experience for you, clarifying all the things that you may not have truly comprehended up until this moment.

The Law of Attraction is a precious gift handed over to you generously so as to change your life. You need to stay focused, and study all the aspects of how to make it work for you based on your own specialized requirements. Now that you have covered the principles of how manifesting works through reading my book, you are ready to transform your existence, and enjoy all the blessings that you have been desiring to receive. This is a spectacular opportunity for you, and you need to dive right in to relish all those glorious benefits ahead.

You have already taken the first step. Congratulations are in order for taking initiative and getting all the way through this book! This was a fantastic idea, and you have so many wonderful things to look forward to now that you have read through these pages. I will be right there by your side throughout your endeavors: offering my advice to you and supporting your ventures 100%. It is an exciting time that unveils before you, and I am sure that you already have a huge smile on your face.

Remember to love yourself, and believe that you can accomplish everything you set your mind on as long as you align to the energy of the universe. Tune in the frequency you emit so that you attract the exact same things that you want, leaving all those toxic thoughts and people out of reach. They do not belong in your reality—what they do is bring you down and distract you from your path. You do not want that: you do not have the time to withhold your manifestations.

Moving forward, I would suggest that you take some time to let all this information sink in. After that, lay out your strategy. Plan your next steps, in order for you to remain organized in your manifesting routine. Make use of the meditations that I have shared with you, and experiment with different techniques. This is the best way to see what appeals to you the most. Whatever you do, always keep in mind that the sky's the limit. The universe is always listening: thus, you should connect with the world, and let abundance overflow your presence.

Welcome to the magnificent world of the Law of Attraction. I am certain that you are flying over the moon already in anticipation of what is about to happen. Believe me, reality will only make you happier. Stay blessed, stay positive, and enjoy life!

REFERENCES

Anthony, K. (2017, December). *EFT Tapping*. Healthline; Healthline Media. https://www.healthline.com/health/eft-tapping

Cartwright, M. (2018, May 16). *Yin and Yang*. Ancient History Encyclopedia; Ancient History Encyclopedia. https://www.ancient.eu/Yin_and_Yang/

congerdesign. (2018). Heart Red Rope. In *Pixabay*. https://pixabay.com/photos/heart-red-rope-loyalty-love-3085515/

Deepak Chopra. (1994). *The seven spiritual laws of success: a practical guide to the fulfillment of your dreams*. Amber-Allen Pub.

Dieter44. (2018). Gem Citrine Stone Jewel Crystal. In *Pixabay*. https://pixabay.com/photos/gem-citrine-stone-jewel-crystal-3569938/

Emma Claire Donovan. (2019, January 16). *The Benefits of TRE for Stress, Anxiety, and Trauma*. Emma Donovan. https://emmaclairedonovan.com/2019/01/16/the-benefits-of-tre-for-stress-anxiety-and-trauma/

Free-Photos. (2014). Tea Cup Rest Afternoon. In *Pixabay*. https://pixabay.com/photos/tea-cup-rest-calm-afternoon-381235/

Free_Photos. (2015). Girl Blonde Sitting. In *Pixabay*. https://pixabay.com/photos/girl-blonde-sitting-lakeside-water-984065/

Gollwitzer, P. M., & Sheeran, P. (2006, January 1). *Implementation Intentions and Goal Achievement: A Meta-analysis of Effects and Processes.*

ScienceDirect; Academic Press. https://www.sciencedirect.com/science/article/pii/S0065260106380021

Good Interactive. (2014). Woman Person Sunset. In *Pixabay*. https://pixabay.com/photos/woman-person-sunset-dreams-alone-491623/

JacksonDavid. (2020). Woman Inspiration Dance. In *Pixabay*. https://pixabay.com/photos/woman-inspiration-dance-model-4775733/

Jaffe, E. (2011). Mirror Neurons: How We Reflect on Behavior. *APS Observer, 20*(5). https://www.psychologicalscience.org/observer/mirror-neurons-how-we-reflect-on-behavior

Jung, J. Y., Oh, Y. H., Oh, K. S., Suh, D. W., Shin, Y. C., & Kim, H. J. (2007). Positive-Thinking and Life Satisfaction amongst Koreans. *Yonsei Medical Journal, 48*(3), 371. https://doi.org/10.3349/ymj.2007.48.3.371

Justasurferdude. (2017). Rose Flower Wiltered. In *Pixabay*. https://pixabay.com/photos/rose-flower-wilted-floral-plant-2335203/

kalyanayahaluwo. (2020). Meditate Meditation Woman Mountains. In *Pixabay*. https://pixabay.com/photos/meditate-meditation-woman-mountains-5375835/

ktphotography. (2017). Candles Bright Light. In *Pixabay*. https://pixabay.com/photos/candles-bright-light-flame-2550688/

Marlene, C. (2018, July 29). *Ithaka: Journey not Destination*. Cheryl Marlene. https://www.cherylmarlene.com/ithaka-journey-not-destination/

Myriams-Fotos. (2017). Woman Beauty Rock. In *Pixabay*. https://pixabay.com/photos/woman-beauty-rock-sea-clouds-2724966/

petig. (2020). Sunset Woman Freedom. In *Pixabay*. https://pixabay.com/photos/sunset-woman-freedom-silhouette-5238044/

Pexels. (2016). Meditate Meditation Peaceful. In *Pixabay*. https://pixabay.com/photos/meditate-meditation-peaceful-1851165/

PIRO4D. (2016). Feng Shui Zen Stones. In *Pixabay*. https://pixabay.com/photos/feng-shui-zen-stones-texture-1927590/

Pitkanen, M. (2018, June). *(PDF) The experiments of Masaru Emoto with emotional imprinting of water*. ResearchGate. https://www.researchgate.net/publication/335909571_The_experiments_of_Masaru_Emoto_with_emotional_imprinting_of_water qimono. (2018). Drop Splash Drip. In *Pixabay*. https://pixabay.com/photos/drop-splash-drip-water-liquid-wet-3698073/

Smith, J. (2018, February 14). *The Emotional Vibration Analysis Frequency Chart*. Blisspot. https://blisspot.com/blogs/5719/654/the-emotional-vibration-analysis-frequency-chart

stokpic. (2015). Woman Working Bed. In *Pixabay*. https://pixabay.com/photos/woman-working-bed-laptop-typing-731894/

Valiphotos. (2015). Road Forest Season. In *Pixabay*. https://pixabay.com/photos/road-forest-season-autumn-fall-1072823/

Wikipedia Contributors. (2019, September 27). *All You Need Is Love*. Wikipedia; Wikimedia Foundation. https://en.wikipedia.org/wiki/All_You_Need_Is_Love

ॐ II ॐ

FEMININE ENERGY AWAKENING

Goddess Energy Secrets & How to Step into Your Divine Power

FEMININE ENERGY AWAKENING: PREFACE

If you're tired of not being looked at as the goddess that YOU ARE, then keep reading. If you have been suppressed for ages and want to step into your power, then keep reading. Are you endlessly giving away your power to other people? Do you often withhold parts of yourself that you wish you could express, judge yourself and feel ashamed? The number one element that will strip you away from your divine magic and power is feeling ashamed. Your life-bearing energy has been suppressed for far too long. It's time to speak your truth.

It is not by chance that you clicked on this book, especially before making the big life decision you are thinking about making. Your magic, your wisdom, your life-giving energy has been covered up and hidden from the world. As women, we all naturally have this magic inside of us, we are creators of the material world, we are the creatrixes.

Are you ready to remember the magic you have inside of you? Are you ready to connect to the self love you need to heal yourself? Women don't just birth children, we birth all of creation into existence. You have been suppressed for far too long and we have been looked at as less than men. Just take a look at the society around you. There are so many demeaning places for women, where they are made to feel as though they are nothing or that their natural, sensual and sacred femininity is something to be ashamed of and used for the benefit of men. Has society conditioned you to suppress and shame the divine sensual part of yourself? You are allowed to tap into that energy again and express yourself how you damn well please.

It is not by chance that you clicked on this page. Perhaps you have incarnated into this being to break the paradigm of how society views and shames women. Most of us don't realize the magic and the power that we hold inside our souls. We are all goddesses and our bodies are our sacred temples. Are you tired of your patterns of being a doormat and not moving forward on your path to your authentic self? You have forgotten your power and that you are a vessel of the divine.

We are ushering in a new world together. By tearing each other down, breaking each other apart, judging and competing with one another, we are suppressing the forthcoming of a new golden age. Come back into the divine feminine cycle of creation. We are supposed to be respected as women and we have to reclaim that power. When you reclaim your power, you stop giving it away to other people. Society has tricked us into giving away our power and not feeling as powerful as we should. We are the rainbow bridge between matter and the spirit world. Tap back into that magic. Reclaim your power.

In this book you will discover:

How to replace or balance masculine traits with feminine traits

Feminine energy awakening secrets that will appeal to younger and more mature women alike

Great hints and exercises, a pre-planned morning ritual to follow and the most incredible, life changing trauma release secrets which you can start applying to clear what no longer serves you today.

This book is designed to empower you even if you've never read a spiritual book before, or if you have failed time and time again to awaken your divine feminine energy in the past. This is because there is room for ALL of us to rise. We must follow the simple and direct path to our awakening. There is no competition between us, we are all one.

So if you want to reclaim your power to heal the world and the patriarchal wounds that have been caused by us all living in a predominantly masculine society for so long then read on. This is a book for all women, no matter your age, stage of life, or your situation. Whether you are hoping to find some way of finding peace and balance within yourself or wanting to step into your warrior goddess power. So if you want to access new depths of self-love, acceptance, inner strength, clarity, and step into a more complete and empowered relationship with yourself then read on. If you want to become empowered & tap into your warrior goddess energy then turn the first page.

INTRODUCTION

Welcome to my book, dear feminine readers! I am so happy to see you landing here, as this means that your instinct and inner power have made you question everything in life. You might have experienced several signs of awakening your divine feminine energy, so you are trying to fill in the gaps and see what lies ahead. There are many other women like you, trying to figure out what to do with that constant urge to discover more about their past, as well as their present and future. By taking part in this awakening, you connect to the universe and find your place in the world. So eventually, you stop wondering about your purpose in life and stop questioning your power.

Have you awakened your divine feminine energy, implementing it in your life? Or, have you ever felt powerless and without a voice, in pursuit of something to support your claims and have your back? Why would you need to depend on others, when you can claim what is yours and receive everything that has been taken from you? Divine feminine energy is what drives women to grandeur. Flowing from within, it expands and releases its uniqueness into the world and the universe. Without it, you feel like you are in hibernation. No one wants to stay like this forever, unable to move and act, reclaiming what they have lost.

In my perception, you are in fact not living your best life, unless you are already healing yourself. This feminine energy which flows from within you can help you heal the wounds and feel reborn. If you are wondering how to elevate your life, how to truly discover what you are made of and claim what has been yours all along, then this awakening of your inner goddess is the best way to go. Until now, you have been missing out for not acting on intuition. There are a plethora of benefits deriving from this awakening process, enabling you to open yourself to the universe and fully perceive the meaning of the world. As a woman, you are a healer. So you need to step up and accept the purpose with which you have been blessed.

It is true that you have been suppressed for years and years on end. As a woman, you have suffered through injustice and you have been stripped of your extraordinary nature. All these elements that have made you exactly who you are, have now been suppressed and you have hidden them deep inside. However, it is time to open your eyes and realize that your identity is to be cherished, rather than persecuted. Patriarchy could not have been more wrong. Women are sacred, and this is how they are supposed to be treated.

AMAZING BENEFITS LIE AHEAD

There are literally endless benefits to harnessing Goddess Energy, so I urge you to continue reading this book. You will discover so much about who you are, what you are meant to do in life, how to cope with challenges, and how to improve your relationships with others and yourself. It will help you to understand the basic terminology, while it will help you dig deeper within your soul to find the answers you have been looking for. This book is going to show you how to trigger these changes in your life, from the standpoint of a woman who needs to comprehend the universe. Of course, you must keep reading to discover the secrets inside!

If you have experienced shame and fear, you need to awaken your feminine energy. Assuming that you have wasted countless years trying to find out more about your purpose in life, you will see the light at the end of the tunnel. You will eventually find your place in the world, which offers closure and ignites wonderful emotions deep within your soul. If you have been feeling insecure, worthless, not enough to please others and stand by their side, then this book will show you the truth. You are divine. Everyone else should be proud and feel privileged just to be around you.

Find out what this power means to you, how it will affect your life and take you to the highest level of awareness. See through the signs and comprehend the meaning of being a Starseed, a wise soul with thousands of lives and countless incarnations with the sole purpose to help and support others. These entities are so powerful and wise, while at the same time, so blissfully ignorant and filled with hopes and dreams. Discover how you can reach out to other like minded individuals, possibly getting closer to your soul family.

At the same time, in this book you will learn how to avoid wasting your feminine energy. Why do you do that? How can you stop? Read through the tips and experiential advice that comes straight from the heart, so that you will know what to avoid. Your energy is divine and exquisite, so you should not waste it without purpose. You should not throw it away to those who do not appreciate it, feeling drained and unappreciated. Instead, you will learn how to preserve and protect your energy. This is your very essence, after all.

Coming to terms with your sexual awareness is definitely one of the most wonderful benefits you will get from reading this book. Are you feeling disappointed by your sex life? Do you just ignore your desires, sinking in a self loathing that prevents you from truly letting go and surrendering to pure joy? You will find out why it is imperative that you stop suppressing yourself. It is in your power to regain control of your body and use it as a vessel to feel utter pleasure. No taboos, no second thoughts, no self doubts. Then, letting go of trauma is truly helpful and can offer you some closure. Despite what has happened during childhood, you cannot drown in the same negative thoughts forever. Instead, you need to take matters into your hands and do what is best for you long term. You should encounter your fears, which is exactly what I am going to show you in this book.

Meditations are truly amazing, versatile and uplifting. Don't you know how to practice them? You shouldn't worry, since I have created some cool meditations to cover your needs. Feel free to try them out and see for yourself if they work like a charm—I am positive they will! And finally, after having grasped what feminine energy is all about and how you can ignite it, you will have the chance to attract everything you have been craving for in life. How does that sound?

Discovering My Own Divine Feminine Energy

I was not born knowing about my divine feminine energy, although my gift has always made me wonder if there is something more than what meets the eye in my life. In fact, I had been rejecting my feminine energy, if I look back at the way I lived my life. My career was so demanding and stressful that it made me build a masculine shell to protect myself against the patriarchal society which dominated my professional life. Due to my competitiveness, I had focused on manifesting mainly masculine traits, so that I would become equal to men. This is pretty much what most modern women strive for, isn't that right?

Let me tell you a little bit about myself and my journey. In my life,

I have been blessed with a caring partner and wonderful friends, as well as a beautiful house and a vibrant lifestyle. I have always felt lucky, along with my ability to overcome the hardships and demanding challenges at work. After all, I always delivered and this was something that filled me with pride and satisfaction. However, as time went by and I evolved, I found it hard to stop and appreciate the moment. I was often left hungry for more, always in pursuit of new thrills. Suddenly, what had kept me going that far was not enough.

Even though I came across as strong and powerful, this was not what I really believed about myself. On the contrary, I second guessed pretty much everything I did, every decision I made. My confidence was gone, undermined by my worries that I would be found lacking and ridiculed by others. Just the thought of being outranked at the office filled me with terror. So I tried to figure out what was wrong. I tried to analyze the emotions that emerged out of the blue, spoiling all the hard efforts that I have made to get to the top—or so I thought. Soon, believe it or not, I stumbled upon the magic of her divine feminine energy and it has affected my own life in more ways than I can describe.

I had some breakthroughs, as past memories appeared right in front of my very eyes, leaving me at awe. Although at first I chose denial as my defensive mechanism, I eventually became more aware of what was happening. I felt my inner goddess calling. As I closed my eyes, I would travel to mystical places far away and out of our dimension. I listened to my body and my divine feminine energy, as I evolved into the sacred creature that I am. All my fears and doubts vanished into thin air. It was very hard for me to do that, but I came to accept all the facades of my journey. My journey has brought me here, trying to pass on my hard earned knowledge and wisdom to you.

You should know that I truly appreciate you choosing to read what I have to say. All this information I have gathered here is a result of my yearning to explore my inner self and reach my highest level of awareness. I hope you find your purpose, like I have found mine. And I truly hope we meet again, after you have opened yourself to this new transcendental experience that is going to shift your mindset once and for all. Happy reading and enjoy, everyone!

❧ I ❧

THE HIDDEN DIVINE POWER
WITHIN YOU

I t is not your fault that you have forgotten what it is like to communicate with your divine feminine. Your inner goddess is not accessible for a reason. Living in a predominantly masculine society for so long has caused patriarchal wounds and covered up the divine feminine power we each have inside of each of us. Our society has negatively conditioned us to believe that female sensuality, natural being, sexuality and expression of oneself is something that should be looked down upon or shamed, when in reality, we are goddesses and SHOULD express ourselves how we please. There is no right or wrong, there is no such thing as restriction and shame, hesitation and doubt, in your book. You are a woman and you are holding the power to rule the world.

Society has tricked us into giving away our power and not feeling as powerful as we should. Women were meant to rule the world, through love and compassion. There are extraordinary elements in feminine energy that make women exceptional leaders, as well as influencers and mentors. A woman can inspire and affect others, guide them through the most challenging situations and provide care, nourishment and unconditional love. These components are unique, ideal for any society. However, things have changed dramatically over the years and now women have been stripped of their own power and uniqueness.

In order to survive, women have been forced to shed their own skin and transform into something that doesn't quite reflect who they really are. Could you ever imagine what a peacock would feel, if they cut down their tail? This would be against their nature, so the peacock would most likely stay shocked for a long time, unable to process what has been done. It is similar to what happens to a woman, once she is deprived of her distinctive traits. She doesn't even recognize herself, since she has associated her very existence with some of these characteristics. Still, over the years, women have survived and have managed to change their standpoint. They have created the foundations to reveal their inner power to the world. And this has not always been easy to accomplish.

Women have learned the hard way that being feminine is not something to take lightly. These components have been fought against for ages, mainly from men who felt threatened by the overwhelming power of women. In combination with their own lack of confidence, men decided to oppose the dominance of the female gender. Women would be persecuted and punished for their very being. It was mayhem, and the repercussions have been mind blowing. It still feels like witch hunting, against those women who have a solid and ambitious vision in their life. Even though we live in a modern society and most stereotypes have vanished into thin air, there are some things that are more resistant to change. Nonetheless, this doesn't mean that we should give up trying.

It is essential to reclaim your power to heal the world and the patriarchal wounds that have been caused by us all living in a predominantly masculine society for so long. This is not going to be easy. It will require time, hard work and patience. But it is inevitable. Justice will be restored, and the rights which have been deprived of females all over the globe will be returned. You deserve to feel powerful and to release that power without any hesitation. It is magical, so you are entitled to that transcendental experience, which will change your life forever.

THE MAGIC OF FEMININITY

When we think of masculinity, we always focus on the end goal. In this way, we are able to measure the results and evaluate masculine behavior. However, with femininity things are quite different. A feminine way of behavior concentrates mainly on the experience. It is far more sensitive and deals with an issue, from the perspective of compassion, creativity and all these fabulous concepts. Unlike masculinity, though, it cannot be measured. So how can you value femininity, when you cannot quantify its results?

For years and years, femininity has been degraded and looked down on, as if it were inferior to masculinity. Most women have been forced to put their feminine traits aside, so that they would become more competitive in the world and seek to which they were entitled. *"This is a man's world"*, right? Instead of letting our guard down and allowing our feelings to take control, we women have felt suppressed for far too long. We have been judged unworthy to what we have been doing, rather than what we were supposed to be. It is a slippery slope here, introducing self-fulfilling prophecy into the mix. According to that socio-psychological phenomenon, an individual is prone to predict certain behavioral patterns and then stick to them, in a form of validating their beliefs (Wikipedia Contributors, 2019).

But why would anyone reject their feminine side? It is part of their inner balance, just like it is represented in the Yin and Yang symbol (Peterson, 2020). Even though the different traits may come across as entirely opposite, in reality they are interdependent and complement one another. This is the concept of dualism, with a perpetual flow balancing each entity. A woman should embrace masculinity, in order to pursue one of her goals. Still, at the same time she should celebrate her femininity. This is what enables her to enjoy things and experiences, even without any apparent gain.

A widespread misconception about femininity is being directly associated with gender. This could not be further from the truth. As discussed above, there are both feminine and masculine components within every single one of us. Nevertheless, in a patriarchal society, the feminine components have been diminished. Their value has been depleted. Instead, masculine traits are what matter the most. When a man focuses on his feminine side, all the world misunderstands him. There is no room for feminine traits, which are considered to be weaknesses. So this misconception has led to women in constant struggle to imitate men and withhold their own power.

Feminine power is irreversible, though. It is unending and includes the entire universe. A feminine is a healer, a nurturer, a caregiver, she creates and supports, she uses empathy and affection. These are elements that should be celebrated, instead of being hunted down and criticized heavily. Women throughout the centuries have contributed to the improvement of the world as we know it, whether or not their contribution has actually been recognized by society. A distinctive example of reality distortion and lack of appreciation when it comes to female contribution is related to Mary Magdalene.

The Example of Mary Magdalene

Are you sure you know the actual story of Mary Magdalene? Or maybe you have been tricked into thinking that she was a prostitute, lacking morality and purpose in life? The truth is that Mary Magdalene was trained under the wings of Isis. She then played an important role in the life of Jesus, teaching him about sexual alchemy and allowing him to overcome boundaries in the physical world. No wonder that she, of all people, is present in His Resurrection! She bears witness to Jesus having risen from the dead to join his Holy Father up in Heaven, and she contributes greatly to the foundation of Christianity.

However, the Church was not very kind to Mary Magdalene. In fact, most people associated her with being a whore, a woman of no value. She was a sinner, according to the Books. Jesus forgave her and showed her the virtuous way of living. But is this really what happened? From our understanding, this is hardly the case. Mary was a powerful woman, who belonged to no one and charted her own course. This is why, unlike most women of her time, you will not see "of X" following her name. Typically, X would be the masculine name, which revealed who the woman belonged to back in the day. Women were the property of men, which pervaded every aspect of their life, including their names. In Mary Magdalene, you will find her origin (being from the famous fishing town of Magdala). She traveled with Jesus, and helped spread his word. Does this sound like a woman of no value?

The Church may have changed her story's facts to suppress women, branding Mary a harlot. Nonetheless, she was a sacred priestess with great power and influence. Mary was independent and guided Jesus, supporting and nurturing him. There is no doubt that Jesus thought highly of her, otherwise she would not be included in his inner circle. Even in the difficult times of pain and suffering, Jesus chose her to remain by his mother's side. This shows just how much he trusted Mary and had faith in her. This theory is in alignment with Dan Brown's novel *The Da Vinci Code* (netage, n.d.). In this case, Mary was depicted as the wife of Jesus Christ.

Moving past myth and religious beliefs, it is safe to assume that Mary was considered dangerous to a patriarchal society. She was strong and did not hesitate to project her power. In fact, she held a special position in the life of a prominent personality—Jesus. Unlike most of the women of her time, she did not compromise her beliefs. Instead, she took a stand and was judged. Maybe the accusations that she was a woman of no honor reflect the profound urge of men to discredit her. Otherwise, a female would replace them and this was something they could not stand.

It is a shame that Mary Magdalene has not received her fair share of universal recognition. More people should know what really happened. More people should be grateful for Mary Magdalene, as she paved the way for other women to stand up and claim their rights. On the contrary, her presence remains ambiguous through the years. It is very difficult for a patriarchal society to admit to having been outranked by a female. Nevertheless, in the philosophy of Jesus, women have always been cherished and their value has never been questioned.

℘ 2 ℘

TAPPING INTO YOUR DIVINE
ENERGY TO HEAL YOUR SHAME

I totally understand why you choose to hold back on your personal self expression because I've been there. Actually, I have been shamed in the past for my sexuality, and for being who I am. My self confidence did not come overnight. It is a work in progress, with its ups and downs, as with every journey. Believing in myself and celebrating my individuality has been my end goal, which I finally reached through awakening my divine energy. Only by realizing that I am unique and amazing and sacred did I get the chance to overcome my fears, and free myself from prejudice and fear.

When I was a teenager, I experienced body shaming. I was rather developed for my age, meaning that my body was quite different from those of other girls. Adolescence can be really cruel for girls, because you see all these radical changes occurring and you can do nothing to stop them. You are in a rollercoaster of emotions, while at the same time your body is changing rapidly. This can be really disappointing, because it prevents you from fitting in and showing the rest of the world that you are like them. You need to belong, but my body made it difficult for that to happen.

Obviously, there was nothing I could do about the changes that took place on my body, other than wear baggy clothes and feel horrible. Instead of finding support among my peers, I found that most classmates would make fun of me and shame me for my body. Interestingly enough, many of them were females. Instead of sticking up for me and accepting me for who I was, they criticized me for no reason and cast me aside. As a result, I eventually started wearing provocative clothes that did not hide my body anymore. On the contrary, I chose outfits that highlighted my curves and revealed that I was sexy and all grown up. Unlike what I believed, this did not have the effects that I would have hoped for. It made my classmates strike even harder, shame me for my self expression and my sexuality. It was a lose-lose situation for me throughout high school.

I spent years trying to come to terms with my body and my own sensuality—until I eventually realized the truth. You see, no one should be judged or looked down on based on what they wear, what they look like, how they behave. Both my former and latter behavior derived from my insecurity and my eagerness to be part of a team. I was innocent and did my best, discovering what I really wanted in life. Being a teen comes with heavy baggage and being shamed only made things worse. It pushed me further from my goal of trying to understand who I am. But my actions were well within my rights, no matter what. It is my body, so I should wear the clothes that make me feel happy and comfortable. It doesn't matter if my breasts are big or small, if I am fat or thin, if my skin is perfect or not. Being shamed took its toll on me, making me an introvert and creating traumas that I have been trying to heal ever since. All that because of shame.

Shame emerges from comparing yourself to your standards and falling short. But where have these standards come from? It is society that dictates what we must do, how we must behave, what we must avoid at all costs. According to society, some behavioral patterns are acceptable, whereas others should be criticized. In order to avoid feeling isolated and left behind, we tend to comply fully with these directives. No matter if we feel like expressing ourselves in a different manner, we end up being exactly the same as everyone else. We do that to avoid embarrassment and social isolation. And these standards are both conscious and subconscious, with the subconscious being even harder to deal with. How can you address a problem, when you don't even know it's there?

Overcoming shame is one of the best things to experience in life. You feel like a huge weight is lifted off your shoulders. Unfortunately, it takes a lot of time for an individual to move past the initial shame and discover how to feel happy again. You do not deserve that burden. You do not deserve to feel like less of a person, just because you are different. Every person is unique and your divine energy is here to remind you of that. Rather than feeling inferior to others, you should really celebrate your difference. This reflects just how wonderful you are, how unique and amazing. To do that, you must get in touch with your feminine energy.

WHAT IS FEMININE ENERGY AND HOW TO ACTIVATE IT?

Many people associate feminine energy with gender. However, this is far from the truth. In fact, an individual is in need of the perfect balance between masculine and feminine traits. When we talk about the masculine energy, we talk about logic and achieving goals. It is more utilitarian, which is great. On the other hand, we refer to feminine energy as the energy creating life. It focuses on beauty, without necessarily being associated with practicality. Both masculine and feminine energy need to be in balance, offering the individual a complete personality to cherish.

Some of the fundamental characteristics of feminine energy are insight, intuition, forgiveness, openness, harmony, sensuality and creativity. You feel the need to indulge in pure enjoyment when doing things in life, rather than evaluate them based on how beneficial they can be to you. Let's think of it this way. When you make yourself a cup of coffee in the morning, why do you do that? If it is because you want to wake up and you know your brain will get stimulated by the aromas of the coffee brewing and the distinctive taste, then you have activated your masculine energy. On the contrary, if you make coffee because you enjoy drinking it, then you are driven by your feminine energy. You know that something sparks joy in your life and you indulge in it, going deeper into the beauty of even the slightest action.

Feminine energy is all about connecting with nature. We are in absolute alignment with the universe, so we need to really listen and connect to nature, rather than go against it. We women are healers, embodying divinity. Feminine energy is nurturing and caring, it holds the formless potential to accomplish everything that we have ever set our minds on. That type of energy moves through life flowing effort-lessly, as life is flowing right through our body. It is that precious harmony we all seek in life. You feel it within you, expanding and releasing its power into the world.

It is not easy to activate feminine energy, even if you have fully comprehended its magnitude. The truth is that in a patriarchal society, this very energy has been pushed aside for thousands of years. We have suppressed feminine characteristics, in favor of masculine ones that make us look stronger and invincible. In order to awaken feminine energy, you must become balanced and come to terms with your inner rhythm. You need your inner vibe, the special movement starting from within. An excellent way to achieve that is through drumming. It doesn't matter what kind of drum you use. Just find one that vibrates and offers you the opportunity to tap on it and produce the rhythm that will awaken you.

What you need to do is connect the rhythm you produce with your heartbeat. Just boom, boom, boom while breathing and becoming aware of your own special vibe will give you the opportunity to activate your feminine energy. You will feel it flowing through your veins, surrounding you in a warm and soft manner. Alternatively, you can use activation meditations, such as Shamana drumming. But no matter what you do, make sure you stay relaxed and focus on your breathing. This is one of the basic things you need to do, so as to align your body and soul to the world. Feel your breathing, control it, feel relaxed and listen to your inner rhythm.

Create an inspiring and calming atmosphere. Activating your feminine energy requires time and effort. You need to be comfortable within your surroundings, so as to promote that change to take place. Turn off the lights, because darkness is able to awaken the energy through eliminating distractions. Artificial lights can keep you at a distance, so you should get closer to nature by keeping all your lights turned off. If you are home, you can energize your body by walking back and forth. This creates the vibrations you need. You can light a candle to add some mysticism into the air, be inspired by the soothing fragrances and drive your inner energy to expand. To acquire harmony, try dancing and drumming. This will allow you to feel the rhythm, feel the vibe bursting from within. Listen to that rhythm and go with the flow. You have now connected to your feminine energy, activating it to show you the way. Obviously, the idyllic ambiance in the dark would not be complete without your external connection to the moon. Go out and look at the stars and the moon, taking in the fresh air and relishing absolute calmness all around you. Finally, engage in some stretching to tone your muscles and flex your body. This is your vessel to activate feminine energy and manifest it, so prepare that vessel properly.

Self Esteem Raising Exercises to Implement

You can tap into your divine feminine energy to heal this shame. Restore your self esteem and your lost confidence in a caring and nurturing manner. Your greatest shame and deepest traumas can actually be a blessing in disguise as these painful elements can actually trigger your awakening. With suffering and darkness comes a break-through.

It takes time to transform your beliefs and start blooming from within. Change cannot happen overnight. It is true that we have grown up with our own insecurities. And we have a bunch of them. We have been programmed to try and fit in, rather than stand out. This is why we tend to doubt and second guess our value. In our attempt to enjoy feminine energy awakening, we need to reverse the situation. Below, I am going to show you some tools, which will help you unveil your uniqueness. If you add them to your daily routine as parts of your morning ritual, you will notice a huge difference over time.

First of all, you should add affirmations everyday as part of your training to awaken your inner power. Affirmations are sentences we use to train our mind into changing our point of view. So if you have been used to looking down on yourself, this has got to change. Time to see yourself for who you really are. It is important to understand that you should be cherished and appreciated. Before moving forward with your exploration of your inner self, you need to acknowledge several things. You are allowed to fail. This is one of the basic acknowledgments in life. Failure is part of living and maturing. All the important people have failed in the past, prior to gaining recognition and leaving their mark in the world.

Then, it goes without even saying that you should stop seeking validation. Why would you care what other people think of you? This will only make you crave more positive feedback and depend on that. On the contrary, you should learn how to be independent and powerful. There is no one supporting you in your life more than yourself. You need to be your biggest fan, so you needn't listen to anyone else. If you believe that something is right, then go for it. Trust your instinct, trust what you think rather than what others believe.

Judgment and criticism have no room in your life. Which leads us to our next acknowledgment. Stay away from toxic people. These are the people who always frown on you and leave you bitter. People who think of their personal gain only and who act according to their interests. These people take pleasure in bringing you down, reducing your value, and making you feel bad about yourself. They feast on your unhappiness, which is an absolutely horrible thing to do. Well, guess what. These people don't belong in your life, so you should do your best to get rid of them as soon as possible.

Having said that, you can identify the issues that are dragging you down. For instance, you may think you look ugly. You might believe you are not smart enough, tall enough, successful enough. The list is literally endless. After addressing the real issues, you are ready to begin with the affirmations to work on reversing your beliefs. You will say "I am beautiful", "I am successful", "I am wealthy", "I am healthy" and everything else you need to say. At first, you will feel awkward and uncomfortable during the process. However, as you practice, you will see the difference.

Journaling is another excellent tool you can use, so as to spark your feminine energy. Some people believe in the visual representation of things. If you are one of them, then you will find the idea of keeping a journal extremely useful. You don't have to stress about it. Think of it this way. Sometimes, we have so much information in our mind that it is too hard to keep everything inside. You feel overwhelmed by this data which you cannot process adequately since they are flooding your brain. Through the journal, you can express all you want to in writing. This can be quite cathartic. You spike your creative side and build your organizational skills. Plus, you can track your progress and read through your thoughts anytime you feel like it. You open your body and all the information will flow from within. One especially helpful tip, if you don't know where to start, is to write down a letter from yourself to yourself.

Are you friends with your mirror? If not, too bad! There is an amazing exercise that you can do. You simply need a mirror. Although you can use that in the bathroom, it is preferable to use a hand mirror, so as to adjust the angle and proximity. The problem with our life is that we often neglect to look at ourselves in the mirror. I mean really look—don't just take a momentary glance. So you need to take the mirror and bring it really close to your face, almost touching the tip of your nose. Then, stare right within your eyes. Don't do anything else, just look deep inside your eyes. Don't smile, don't laugh, don't get distracted. You might experience awkwardness, which is totally understandable. You are not used to that level of intimacy with yourself. As soon as you are OK with that, start with your affirmations. You will see that this will shock you. Don't get discouraged if you cry the first time you do this. Soon you will get used to it and the results will be astounding—just like you!

Finally, you need to train your mind not to be bothered by life getting in the way. Obviously, you cannot do that. But bear with me for a moment. Why should you get sad over even the tiniest setback? Why be affected by other people's opinions? This is your life and you should live it exactly the way you want to. So practice not giving a damn about what is going on. Do the things which fill you with joy and satisfaction. Meet with people who make you feel good about yourself and support you all the way. Steer clear of everything that brings you down. You are on the path to greatness, don't forget about that.

❧ 3 ❧
HOW TO STOP GIVING AWAY YOUR
DIVINE FEMININE POWER

Our own existence, the entire world around us, is made of infinite energy from above. This energy is neutral and gets contracted, so as to become matter and create the material world we live in. It gets its physical form and is manifested through our thoughts and feelings, reflecting both our masculine and feminine energy. We need to preserve that energy, stop giving it away, to be happy and accomplished in life. However, this is not an easy task. Energy often flows away and is repelled from bodies, whether or not we are actively aware of it.

Whenever we think about something that is bringing us down, we let our divine feminine power and energy escape us. Take a moment to process that. Imagine that you go out and you have too many cocktails, even though you had convinced yourself that you would limit your alcohol intake to a couple of drinks. You get back home and you start beating yourself up. Thoughts of worthlessness run through your mind, making you feel bad about yourself. You are disappointed and you feel like you are never going to recover from that negative emotion. This is all draining you off your energy. All this self loathing does nothing but keep you diverted from your goals.

The same thing happens with every single thought that you have that brings you down. There are quite a few issues you are dealing with, which can make you feel bad and even lead to depression. If you are unhappy about your finances, if you are let down by your lack of discipline in following a new diet and exercise regime, if you are drawn to the wrong men—all these things drain precious energy. So you need to stop and find ways to protect your feminine energy. You need to prepare yourself to overcome those leaks and hold on to as much energy as possible.

Social anxiety adds to the mix. When you feel uncomfortable and insecure within society, you spend too much energy. Rather than feeling cool and secure in what you are doing, you waste your energy and become exhausted thinking about the consequences. You overanalyze things, you measure the pros and cons, you play scenarios within your head. This is not working out for you. So it is time to break free from this vicious cycle, which has to do with society's opinion about yourself and your value.

As you can imagine, preserving your feminine energy is quintessential for your well being. If you waste that precious energy, it is like you are throwing away your past. All the time spent creating that energy, all the sacrifices that other women have made and that they have suffered, so that you could enjoy the benefits of connecting to your inner goddess, all that would have gone to waste. Are you thinking of denying the very core of your existence? Unless you are on the brink of letting go of your feminine aspect in life, you need to do your best to avoid that. To maintain your divine power, you must treat it with respect and prudence. Do not spend it on thoughts, beliefs, acts, and relationships that do not live up to your standards. If you do, sooner or later you will feel the negative consequences as your energy is running right through you.

CLEAR YOUR DIVINE VESSEL AND RELEASE NEGATIVE ENERGY

There are many different types of people who are wrong for you. They suck you dry and leave you without the tiniest bit of energy. These are the people you don't want in your life, even if at first sight you may think that you do. It is important that you use your feminine energy to protect yourself against narcissists, bad relationship partners, energy vampires, society's judgment and criticism. In this way, you will master the art of preserving your energy and feeling exactly like you are meant to feel—awesome. Detoxification will cleanse your life of unhealthy relationships.

In order for you to clear your divine vessel and release all that negative energy that has been piling up for so long, you need to follow some easy and helpful steps. First off, you must admit that there is too much going on in your life and you are allowing too many people to control you. Does that sound familiar? Why would you ever want to leave the important decisions to others? There is no one who knows what you need better than you. Make sure that you identify these people, who have been sucking the air out of your lungs and remove them from your life.

Set your boundaries so as to avoid wasting your energy. These people will never stop. They will keep on demanding from you as if you are obliged to deliver. What you do and how you live should not concern them. It is not for them to judge and advise you. Nor should they have the power to make your decisions. You are the one in control. It is time to step up onto that pedestal and see the world from a privileged point of view. Then, it is equally important to be selfish and to act in your best interest. Selfishness is not always a bad thing. I am not talking about harming others. Of course not. However, you need to put yourself first and act according to your beliefs, your desires, and your needs. Who else would you want to please? Feel free to pamper yourself, nourish and nurture your body and soul. The happiness you get out of the whole experience is beyond comparison. Plus, it helps you to maintain your feminine energy.

Finally, you need to stop feeling guilty. Guilt is often used to pressure us to act against our will. For example, if you don't want to hang out with a guy, why not confront him and tell him about it? There is no reason for you to prolong the inevitable. In fact, you will be better off without each other, since there is no actual chemistry between you. The same happens when you attend a party that you don't want to, eat food you despise, watch a movie you don't enjoy, and the list goes on and on. Don't apologize for your choices in life. Stand by them and support your decisions. When you apologize, you are contracting your energy. You are pushing it downward, and you feel the pressure. You don't deserve that kind of pressure, so let it go.

When you think about something for too long, you spend energy. For instance, do you recall how many times you longed for love to come along? All this energy is contracted, and you feel tight and suppressed. As a result, you repel what you are looking forward to experiencing—because of that energy contraction. Every time you feel judged or shamed by what you have done, you act in the opposite way from how you would want to act. You are not attracting the things to which you are entitled; you are pushing them away.

So the solution is to release the contraction, by breathing them out and aligning your energy with a higher energy. You get connected to the source energy, since you are more relaxed and you release the tension and the contracted energy flows from within you. There is infinite potential for you out there, as long as you stop limiting yourself. Step out of the consciousness that is not working anymore. Detox your mind and body, by letting go of that suppressed energy.

Activate The Goddess Within

Having released your negative energy, you can now purify your aura to make room for your feminine energy awakening. Are you intrigued to ignite the divine feminine energy from deep inside? Are you ready to activate your goddess from within? You need to put those feminine energy affirmations in your morning ritual, so that you reverse your training and allow your mind to contemplate what you really want to pursue in life. There are several things you should focus on to boost your self awareness and empower your inner divine energy.

You are a goddess and you should start behaving like one. Believe in your power and feel all those positive things that derive from being such a woman. Why are you happy being a female? What makes your heart beat faster? Why would others go out of their way to come a little closer to you? If you think you are not worthy, you need to reconsider. People have gone to extremes because they wanted to do something that they felt motivated to accomplish. They have stayed out in the cold, in really bad weather conditions, risking their life and abstaining from food and water, because they wanted to reach a high mountain top. Others have fought to the death for a beautiful woman, or to defend their family's honor. There is nothing to prevent someone from coming closer to you, even if this means that they would have to sacrifice something to do so.

Are you still undecided as to whether or not you deserve to communicate with your inner goddess? Really, there should be no doubt. However, when you practice the following affirmation, you will come to open your eyes slowly, and truly see what it means to be you. It is much more than a word or two. It is much more than a feeling or two. You are a reflection of the entire universe, living in perfect harmony. You have come to earth to help mankind and to make the world a better place in so many ways. Everything you do has been blessed. Hence, you don't have to justify your actions or ask for anyone's permissions.

First of all, you should remind yourself of your best qualities. "I am loving", "I am self sufficient", "I am a caring person", "I am kind", and "I am loveable" can all serve as an introduction. "I exude love and compassion", "My spiritual energy is high" and "I am a powerful, self accomplished woman" are equally helpful. You need to be able and let down your guard and surrender to the harmony of nature. It is imperative that you relax and open your soul, so as to receive these affirmations and accept their truthfulness. "I am a queen", "I embody my divine energy", "I am in perfect alignment with my ancient power and wisdom"—these are all excellent affirmations to go on with. "I am the force of the wind", "I am an extension of cosmic creation", "I embrace my sensual energy" and "I express myself truthfully, honestly and without haste" are also amazing affirmations to use.

Through these affirmations, you must open your mind and allow your body to receive all the precious gifts it is about to receive. Your inner goddess waits to be released to the cosmos, so you need to prove yourself worthy of receiving that special honor. You must align with the universe and believe in yourself. Without this alignment, you are doomed to keep your goddess hidden and suppressed for all eternity. Believe in the fact that you are extraordinary and pass this on to your subconscious. "My energy is strong and vital", "I am the young, the new, the ancient and the old", "I am a wonderful manifestation of the Divine Feminine"—these affirmations will keep you on track, even when you fall off the wagon and are set astray.

4

CREATING HEAVEN ON EARTH
TOGETHER

Being a woman is a true blessing and it should be considered as such. Over the years, though, women have been shamed and diminished. We have been looked down on for so long that it has nearly become second nature to us. It seems that we are constantly fighting against all odds. In a patriarchal society, being a woman comes with its downside. Nobody is willing to give up on their long-lasting rights. So it is a neverending struggle to prove your worth and earn your place in the world.

This is why we need to stick together. It is us against the world, trying to establish our position in society. Otherwise, we will always be looking over our shoulder, on edge that something is going to creep up behind us and deprive us of whatever we have achieved so far. Isn't that right? We need to make a pledge to help each other and boost our power together. It is our time to rise. As long as we empower one another, we are going to usher in a new golden age which will create heaven on earth where we all can thrive.

Unfortunately, we women have learned the hard way how difficult it is to trust others. Having experienced injustice, you cannot help but remain skeptical all the time. Betrayal is not an unknown world, and it hurts to put yourself out there, exposed to the same threats over and over again. So we have built ourselves a wall, big enough to keep everyone at bay. This can be a great strategy, but it comes with risks. One of the risks that you take is that you may be warding off who can help you. So in your effort to protect yourself (which is absolutely understandable and kudos for that), your wall prevents you from connecting with other women.

However, it is crucial to understand there are more things connecting than dividing us women. Although we come in different shapes and sizes, although we may be miles apart, although our backgrounds vary greatly, it is that special feminine sparkle which brings us together. We are women, meaning that we have achieved greatness through difficult times. This is what defines us. Hardships we have overcome only make us stronger. But they often make us colder towards our own kind. You should not fall for that trap, as it drives you further away from your true essence.

No longer should we tear each other down and judge each other. We are all sacred feminines and we need to start coming together, to remind each other of the magic that we hold inside. When we come together, our energy amplifies and we can send that out to the world to create change. United we stand, divided we fall. It is inevitable that the power comes in numbers. So join a growing network of women and multiply your strength, rather than trying to cause harm.

We are special, you need to wrap your mind around this. The world should be welcoming towards our uniqueness, acknowledging what we are capable of. Nevertheless, reality is much harder. There are obstacles that keep bringing us down. Men seem to have placed us in cages in an attempt to restrain us. Can you imagine what would happen if we were to join forces for the common good? These restraints would be no more. This is our calling, so don't turn your back on it, just because you think that you are better off on your own. You aren't, trust me.

TEMPTED TO TEAR OTHERS DOWN?

There are many people who feel they are obliged to compare themselves to others. When that comparison falls short, there is no other way but to try to diminish the value of the individual who has been proven superior. Does this behavioral pattern seem familiar to you? Are you constantly antagonizing other women? This is not healthy since it prevents you from truly blossoming from within. Instead, you need to focus on your own self, trying to improve and move forward. By wasting your time observing what other people do, you deprive yourself of valuable time spent in personal growth. All these distractions will take their toll on you and leave their scars for good. They will keep you from your true goal and bruise your relationship with your allies.

To be honest, this urge to come across as superior to others might reveal a hard truth for yourself. Perhaps you have been wounded deeply and you now feel compelled to prove your value to yourself and others. Maybe you have not found the recognition that you deserve, and this is something you need to acknowledge before you can resolve it. So the next time that you are about to gossip or judge another person, especially a woman with whom you share many common things, ask yourself this question: what is driving you to behave like this? Is it family, is it your peers who are always judging you for who you are, what you wear, what you do in your life?

If you are tearing down someone else, judging them, or competing with them, then that means you are doing that to yourself. This is a reflection of your own negative emotions. Are you having doubts as to your competence about something? Are you feeling less worthy than what you would have hoped? These doubts might remain subconscious, but they still affect your behavior and spike your insecurity. If you were independent and confident, then you would not spend your time figuring out what others do. You would be too busy trying to perfect your own skills, your performance, your style. This is what you need to aim for. Improve yourself, by figuring out how to stop criticizing others.

So every time you are passing judgment on a female colleague or a friend, a mere acquaintance or a total stranger, try to interpret the signs. Read in between the lines and see what these actions mean. Do you want to be bad towards others? I know this is not the case for you, as a Starseed is never driven by evil. Does that make you feel happy or satisfied in any way? I am sure it doesn't. In fact, it most likely fills you with regret. These actions are clearly not your style. They are most likely a reflection of what you need to heal inside yourself. When you don't like what another woman is doing or don't agree with them, it triggers something inside you that you need to heal.

It is time to unleash your passion and let it guide you, while listening to what your heart dictates. This is the only way for you to start observing things that you have never paid attention to before. There is beauty in the world and in every single one of us. There are infinite ways, in which each of us can live our own lives. In a similar pattern, there are infinite paths we can choose, according to our individual preferences. No right or wrong here, no "one-size-fits-all" solution. It doesn't matter the tiniest bit whether you agree with it or not. You just let everyone be, like they let you—no judgment, no negative vibe, no worries, just pure bliss.

Finding Your Soul Family and Other Starseeds

Do you feel like you don't belong here on earth? Have you ever had a near-death experience or have you ever remembered things that you should not have been able to? Then you are probably experiencing what each Starseed goes through during the unveiling of their true essence. A Starseed is an advanced soul who has arrived on earth from other planets and other dimensions. Your purpose is to help humanity in this difficult time of Ascension in which we are living in. I am sure that explains a lot about your life.

Always drawn by the mysteries of life, science fiction, and space, you are sensitive and empathize with other people's feelings. Most would describe you as a dreamer, probably too aloof at times, and an extrovert, with a yearning to help others. This is your calling, after all. You have decided to visit earth, which shows how caring and affectionate you are. You believe in the highest principles, such as love and solidarity, equality and unconditional help.

However, your transition into a human being came at a substantial cost. The cost was none other than oblivion. You forgot your purpose in life, which made you unaware of the challenges you are about to face. Over time, memories come up and you start connecting the dots. It is like a puzzle and you are meant to find the pieces one by one. Although it can feel exhausting, with every new discovery you get a little closer to your end goal. You get closer to finding out more about your calling, about the real reason why you are here now.

I know that, for a Starseed, it can be really lonely here on earth. You feel misplaced, as if you don't have a place to call home. Above all that, you cannot quite communicate with those around you. No one gets you, not even when they pretend that they do. Wouldn't it be nice to surround yourself with like-minded, awakening beings? People you can share everything with and truly connect to—these are the people that will be your soul family. They are so hard to find, but they will eventually find you or you will find them. The powers drawing you close together are much higher than any obstacles that stand in the way.

Of course, there are no ads you can post to meet other Starseeds and awakened creatures. I wish it were that easy! The truth is that you don't even feel 100% sure that you are a Starseed. You have seen the signs, so you know something is up. You are not like others. But are there others like you? The good thing is that you'll know right away. As soon as you meet another Starseed, you will feel as if you have known each other an entire lifetime. Your instinct will be right, as you have been companions from a different dimension.

Starseeds will most likely have the same interests as you. They will be drawn by space and extraterrestrial life, they will enjoy flying and they will be very sensitive. You will identify your own traits in them. You can improve your social life and intensify your awakening by reaching out to these wonderful people. In fact, you will see that your power becomes much stronger when you are around them. Remember that you have the same positive effect on them, too.

Check out seminars and events relevant with spiritualism. Forums and chat rooms, groups on Facebook and websites can help you out. Attending reading or acting classes, meditation and yoga sessions might also work. A planetarium or a place where you can observe the stars are also amazing places to find other Starseeds. Look for that unique vibe in the air, where you feel like you have found the missing pieces. It is a warm and cozy feeling, a sense of accomplishment. Better yet, you will feel the same thing and share your excitement.

❈ 5 ❈

YOUR SOUL RETURNING FROM
PAST LIFETIMES

T hrough incarnation, we have all been through past lives. We are all in this perpetual journey towards divinity. We choose to come to life as women and the reason for doing so is to get ready for this shift in consciousness. We wish to reconnect with the magic and power with which we have lost touch. Perhaps in a past or parallel life you were executed or condemned for speaking your truth or being a natural healer. You have come back NOW because you can't be killed for this and you can't be silenced anymore.

We came here to remind other women and everyone in the world that we are here to rise and balance out the divine masculine and feminine energies once again, to reclaim our power and heal the world and the patriarchal wounds that have been caused by us all living in a predominantly masculine society for so long. You have come back incarnated in this form ready for the divine feminine energy awakening.

Can you imagine that there was a time when people would hunt us down and kill us, condemning us to a painful death? This would not happen because we had murdered or raped or tortured another human being. Women were only persecuted because men have accused them of witchcraft. Yes, our sacred feminine consciousness due to the inherent ancient connection to the divine feminine has cost us dearly. People burnt us because we were considered evil.

What is evil about holding the power to reach the divine? We were supposed to be protected, worshiped even, because of our connection to divinity. Instead, society wanted to banish us. They would not stop until they had wiped us all clean from the earth. It was a truly bloody persecution, since they would not show any mercy. It was as if they felt threatened by our unique nature. So instead of trying to understand us, they chose to fight. They didn't want to be stripped of their power, and we would prove ourselves worthy of taking up even the greatest challenge.

Fortunately, we have found a way back to claim what is ours. Although we have been persecuted and completely misunderstood throughout history, we have always bounced back, stronger than ever. Throughout history, you will often come across the organized crimes committed against women. Without the tiniest effort to validate the accusations designed to destroy us, men kept on beating. And we kept on taking the punches, getting ready to strike back harder.

Now, our time has come. We need to reverse the current situation and take back what has clearly been stripped from us. We are divine, we are chosen, we are entitled to power and bliss. Why have we waited for so long? It takes time for the wheel to turn. Change cannot happen overnight. We have been waiting patiently, using incarnation to take a female form to claim our rights. And now it is finally time to reap the benefits of our long lasting anticipation.

Are you ready to gain a consciousness of your past lives? Do you feel the urge to truly comprehend what it means to be YOU? If so, you can move forward to the next step. You will be expected to cleanse your inner soul before you delve into the treasures of your past existence. Prior to knowing what has happened to you, it is crucial that you pave the way carefully. Clear your karma from your past lives and prepare yourself to move forward. It is your time to shine, so don't let anything hold you back and drown you in negativity.

CLEARING YOUR KARMA FROM YOUR PAST LIFE

Take a moment to think about a project you have been working on for years. Unless you have set proper foundations, you will soon realize that your entire endeavor might crumble into pieces. It is only fair to assume that you need to be careful when structuring the whole thing. Otherwise, it will probably be a lost cause. Now consider having spent a significant amount of time, only to discover that you have been laboring under an illusion. This can be devastating, to say the least.

The same applies in real life. You cannot expect to move forward unless you have successfully dealt with your past life issues. Anything that has been dragging you down, anything that has been left unresolved, is a ticking time bomb. It may not explode right away, but it will go off eventually. So you should act beforehand and make sure that you have no weights pulling you under. You must be set free from all these issues from your past. This is the only way that you can ever expect to succeed in reaching your divine power.

When you are holding a grudge, you are injuring your karma in a serious way. In a similar pattern, bitterness can hurt you emotionally and prevent you from reaching your divinity. Even though it might sound tempting, you need to steer clear of wishing others ill as they make their way through their life. This is not who you are. Furthermore, you should be grateful for whatever happens. This includes not only the good things, but also the hardships you get through. If something positive comes your way, you are free to enjoy and cherish these moments. On the other hand, when something negative comes your way, be grateful for the challenge. It is a great opportunity to allow you to grow and become more mature.

Negative thoughts are horrible, because they poison you from within. They don't allow you to experience euphoria and relax. Instead, they surround you with unwanted energy. This is not something that you need in your life, so don't invite that energy over. The best thing you can do is let go of negativity. Focus on positive thoughts, optimism and, when in doubt, make a list of all the good things you have in your life. I am sure that they will outweigh the bad things, so you will see the light at the end of the tunnel.

Karma has to do with the actions and reactions that choices bring in your life. If you have been treating others like garbage, you cannot expect the universe to treat you differently. So in order to clear your karma, it is best to filter your behavior and evaluate it accordingly. Be nice to people, smile and treat them with respect. Being loving and caring is never out of fashion. In this way, you will get rid of all the clutter that you are dealing with emotionally and spiritually.

Finally, I cannot stress enough the importance of forgiving others. Sometimes, it is hard to do that. There are behaviors you cannot ignore. People can be very hard and cruel. But vengeance will only make things worse. You will keep on feeling bitter inside since you will never get closure. On the contrary, you will repeat the same scenario all over again, thinking of what has driven you to feel that way. You do not deserve to be stuck in that position. So get over it, forgive, and get rid of what has been burdening you.

Now that you have cleansed the past, it is time to dive deep into our past lives. A wonderful way to do that is through Past Life Regression Therapy. This can work wonders for you, assuming that you have fully comprehended what you are made of. In other words, you need to have completed clearing your karma and, of course, you must have come to terms with being a Starseed. Are you excited? I know I am. Let's move on to the next step, shall we?

Past Life Regression

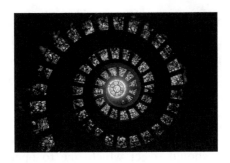

Past Life Regression will guide you towards discovering hidden secrets about your past lives. You have had thousands of them, so it is only fair that you learn more about how you have lived throughout eternity. However, you cannot simply ask and receive. The process is a little more complicated. First, you need to clear your mind completely. Before you get this shift of consciousness, you must make sure that the conditions are ideal. You don't want any distractions interrupting you from your anticipated journey, do you?

Pick a place where you feel comfortable. This will most likely be your home, but you can select another place, if you prefer. Then, wear something that you hardly notice. Cozy pyjamas, a T-shirt and yoga pants or leggings are fine. Just remember that you should clear your mind from any distractions, including those coming from your surrounding environment. Feel the temperature in the room you have selected. Is it too cold or too hot? Are there any bad smells that can set you off course during your session?

After having created the perfect atmosphere, you will need to sit down comfortably and close your eyes. If you want, you can have some relaxing music in the background, as well as lightly scented candles or sticks. It is important to be alone with your thoughts. Now keep your eyes closed and get rid of the tension. Dispose of any thoughts that have been troubling you. Now is your time to concentrate on your breathing and your breathing alone. Each time you inhale, think of the lotus flower. Every time you exhale, that lotus flower opens up and reveals its true beauty.

Slowly but steadily, you will notice that your breathing becomes deeper. You feel that and nothing else. You have become conscious of your existence, appreciating the moment and living only for that. It is time to let go and ascend far away. Are you ready for that journey? Flying is fun, especially when you leave your body and lift higher above the ground through your light soul. You distance yourself from gravity and absorb everything all around you. It is a sight for sore eyes traveling to a different dimension.

Once you reach your destination, you should choose which past life you are going to delve into. There are doors leading to your past lives, which is why you should select which one to open. As mentioned above, you have been through multiple different lives. Not all of them have been equally important, for sure. Evaluate your needs and preferences, figuring out where you want to go. As soon as you reach your decision, set out to descend back to earth. Observe once more what is going on around you, taking in every single detail. Can you see where you are heading? This is very exciting.

Upon arrival to your past life timeline, you will experience your birth. Do not be afraid of the emotions you are about to feel. They will be intense, but you should cherish them. Try to hold on to these memories, as to what it felt like being born. Was it painful, or was it relaxing and blissful? No matter what, keep your eyes open and observe the details. Are your parents with you? Where are you? In which part of the world are you? Before you know it, your life will be passing you by quickly. Flashcards of the most significant things that happened in your life will be displayed before you and you will need to connect the dots.

Were you a good person? Were you healthy? These are just a few of the questions that you will need to answer throughout your journey. According to your past, you will regain memories that will help you out in your present and future life. This is invaluable information that you would not be able to obtain elsewhere. So gather as many details as possible and try to realize if you were worthy of remembering. The odds are that a Starseed is stellar.

At the big finale, you will need to relive your death. This can be a painful experience, but it is imperative that you don't shy away from the experience. Try to figure out if you had a smooth passing, if you were of age, if you had your loved ones beside you. These are truly precious pieces of information as they have left their imprint deep inside you, even though you may not be able to recall the details. You are looking at your life from a higher perspective. The more you know about who you were, the better. It might seem like you are suffocating, but you will be alright in the end. Good as new, with all the valuable lessons that you have learned along the way.

Now, once you have completed this cycle of wandering through your past life, you will be requested to come back. You cannot stay there forever, since you have already experienced everything within that lifetime. The only thing you can do is use that knowledge to your advantage, becoming even wiser and more mature than before. It is that wisdom that will stay with you from now on, assisting you in your struggle to reach out to your divine nature. You are slowly waking up, embracing your feminine side, and moving on to the next step of awareness.

After having wrapped up the journey, you will ascend once more far away in different dimensions and then you will start your descent to your current life on earth. Enjoy the ride and try to hold on to what you have unveiled throughout this experience. When you open your eyes after the past life regression has ended, you will probably feel shocked. You will feel overwhelmed by your recently acquired knowledge. It is certain that you cannot have anticipated all that. Maybe you never would have expected to have been incarnated as a male figure in the past. Perhaps you had never imagined you would be an artist, a philosopher, a housewife, a carpenter.

First, you ought to deal with the shock and come to terms with whoever you have been in your past life. Then, check out your past behaviors. There are patterns that may interpret your ongoing habits. What would you think about scars that have remained intact with every incarnation of yours? Unresolved issues that pretty much define who you are and how you react. These issues have to be encountered, otherwise they will continue to haunt you. This is why it is so crucial to gather information from your past lives, so that you are able to confront these challenges now. Reprogram yourself and enhance your awareness, gaining more wisdom and finding the resources required to elevate your existence.

The more knowledgeable you get through past life wisdom, the more powerful you become and the more you are able to rise above the challenges that you are bound to face in this life. Live up to your expectations, soar, and show what you are truly made of. You are divine, so don't let anyone tell you otherwise. First and foremost, you must love yourself and believe in your power. If you don't, who will?

❧ 6 ❧

LOVE THY SELF, SKYROCKET
SEXUALITY, AND POUR OUT
INSPIRED CREATIVITY

H ave you been suppressing your feelings for your entire lifetime? Your wounds as a child may have stemmed from other past lives, or they may have resulted from years and years of abuse. This is perfectly understandable, since no one can do something about their past. Children are powerless, fragile and easy to shape. Adults are meant to shield and protect them. However, this is not always the case. Some families are responsible for creating deep wounds that never seem to heal. Children grow up thinking that they are worthless, and that they deserve nothing good in their life.

Traumatized children are on their way to becoming traumatized adults. Endless complexes, feelings of inferiority, and negative thoughts flood their mind. Nevertheless, there is a huge difference between childhood and adulthood. The former comes with an a priori sense of powerlessness. The latter, though, should not be the same. You are a grown up person, capable of making your own decisions. You have the power that it takes to stop that vicious cycle and claim what you are entitled to. There is no room for self pity. Why would you feel sorry for yourself? If something doesn't suit you, change it.

When it comes to emotional stability, old wounds can be very dramatic. They come across as too hard to overcome, drowning you in negativity. As a result, you do not believe in your value and you remain entirely dependent on what others think of you. In the past, it was your father who accused you of being stupid. It was your mother who never showed you affection. It was your classmates who called you names and bullied you. Now who has taken their place? Who is bullying you now?

Self loathing is not for you. You are not the victim here. Even though you may have experienced some negative things in the past, you are fully capable of reversing the situation. Do you believe that you are unworthy? This is something that you need to work on. Otherwise, history will repeat itself and you will find that you are living the same thing over and over again. Take a stand for yourself, take a stand against harassment and honor what you represent. This is your moment, don't forget that.

Being a woman, you understand the feelings you are experiencing, and you are expected to face them. You must release them, so as not to allow them to harm you anymore. No matter how cruel these feelings are, no matter how much pain they put you through, you need to rise up. The only solution to get rid of these negative emotions is to acknowledge them. If you continue to suppress and shove them deep within your soul, you will never feel whole. You will always be lacking something. Dealing with your emotions is quintessential for your well being and understanding of your true value. These emotions are often dark and cold, but still you need to address them, process them and eventually eliminate them.

People who are responsible for your feeling of worthlessness do not belong in your life. Set boundaries and do not fall for the oldest trick in the book. Do not let others determine who you are. Instead, show the world what you stand for and this will be reflected on others. The rest of the world will see you for who you are, paving the way you want them to walk. As you can see, you hold the keys to your freedom, or your captivity. You hold the keys to your happiness, or your misery.

When it comes to romantic relationships, things can get ugly pretty fast. A toxic relationship can poison you, which is something you definitely do not deserve. Why put up with this kind of behavior?

If your significant other doesn't live up to your standards, then you should think twice before letting them occupy such a precious spot in your life. Being your loved one is an honor and he should thank you for that. It is not your place to beg, nor is it to offer one opportunity after the other. A couple must be in perfect alignment with each other, allowing both to blossom and become better. What you need from your relationship is reassurance, safety and love, respect and affection. Does he tick those boxes for you or not?

Assuming that you are having doubts as to the quality of your relationship, you already hold the answer in your hands. Get out of this toxic relationship, before it gets worse. You should feel sure when you are with him, not prolong your insecurity. A man who wants to be in your life will show you with every opportunity he gets, not add to your negative thoughts and fears. Don't settle for anything less than what you are entitled to. You deserve so much and you should not stop until you find that.

Before you know it, you will find your true purpose in life and you will not even recall what the past had brought you. There are people who make a difference and those who come into your life just to prove we are not all the same. Guess who you should aim at introducing in your life! In this book, you will find all the help you need, so as to consider what your passions are and how you can incorporate those into your life. Which are the things that inspire you the most? What do you enjoy doing? You can find intriguing activities, pursue your dreams or experiment with different things in your daily routine. Sooner or later, your passions will emerge.

This is the only way to achieve that healthy balance in your life. Unless you reach the point of self love, you cannot have high hopes. On the contrary, you will compromise and avoid reaching true greatness. All these barriers that appear in the shape of inadequate people will continue taking their toll on you. Are you willing to let them gain control over your life? I don't think so. You are meant for reaching your divinity. So how can you settle for less than that? It is all out there for the taking. You just need to reach out and grab what you want. This will be the beginning of amazing things happening to you.

Once you have found your balance, you will reveal a whole new world of potential. You will get the opportunity to activate, enhance, and skyrocket your sexuality and creativity. You will feel like a whole new different person, ready to take on the world. When you find someone to share this new world with, you will have acquired all the tools you need for making the most out of your relationship. You will no longer be filled with fear or guilt. Contrary to what you may believe about yourself now, you will have clarified that you are awesome and you deserve the whole wide world. All that comes from the inspired process of opening your chakras.

OPEN YOUR CHAKRAS AND LOVE YOURSELF

Are you ready to love yourself? I know, it can be hard at times. Still, remember that you are unique. Think of your journey, all those past lives joined together. This concentrated wisdom deriving from countless lives has become your hard earned possession. You are equipped to face life with confidence, self love and appreciation. Your companion will join you, in an adventure you will both treasure. There is no room for looking back, there is no place for self loathing and endless doubts getting in the way of your happiness.

Open your chakras, so that you enjoy your relationship to the fullest. There are seven chakras you will need to open from your body, improving your energy flow and seeing the benefits in your connection with your significant other. Don't hold back on your sexual pleasure, don't be afraid of releasing that power. You will find that unlocking those parts of your body will help you achieve sexual divinity, gaining control over every inch of your body in a magical, almost transcendental manner.

The first chakra is the root, at the end of your backbone. This signifies the level of trust cultivated between you and your partner. You cannot be with a person you don't trust, can you? Indulge in aromatherapy and burn Muladhara incense, as well as essential oils. Sandalwood, ginger, cypress are all great for that. Repeat affirmations that bring positive effects about safety, in order to develop that sense of security all around you and pass it on to your relationship. "I am safe", "I am not afraid", "The universe will protect me", "I love my body and myself" are just a few of the affirmations you can use, as many times as you feel like it. Practice yoga and focus on postures like the warrior, squad, mountain, or goddess.

The second chakra is sacral, which is all about acceptance. In this case, you will need Svadhisthana incense and essential oils to burn. Chamomile, patchouli, rose are all splendid options. Now you must repeat affirmations, which are relevant to your sensual and creative nature. "I embrace change", "I deserve to experience sexual pleasure and fun", "I feel comfortable in my body" will work amazingly for you. Bound angle and happy baby are the best yoga postures for healing your sacral chakra.

Moving on to your third chakra, which is the solar one and signifies appreciation. This is another crucial element in a relationship. Manipura incense and essential oils are in order here, so choose among cinnamon, musk and saffron. You must repeat affirmations about your own personal power. "I am ambitious", "I am capable of taking on any challenge" and "I will make positive changes in my life" will all help you unblock this chakra. As for yoga postures, go for sun salutations, the warrior posture and the boat.

Obviously, the fourth chakra is one of the fundamentals in love. It is the heart chakra, having to do with the purity of love and affection experienced in the relationship. Orange, jasmine, lavender are all inspiring aromas which work really well for you, since you should burn Anahata incense and essential oils. Affirmations unblocking your heart include "I am open to love", "I love myself and I love all other people" and "I forgive myself and others". Yoga will help you direct your heart towards the sky, so the perfect postures for that are camel, bridge and dog facing upward.

Throat is the fifth chakra, showing positive expression and admiration. A couple should support one another and express their thoughts, respect, and love in a way that heals the soul. Sage, peppermint, and eucalyptus are perfect for burning Vishuddha incense and essential oils. Through affirmations, you should focus on openness in communication. Try "I communicate honestly", "I listen actively" and "I believe in authenticity when communicating". The fish pose, camel, and plow are great yoga postures for you to try out, so as to concentrate on your throat and thyroid.

The third eye chakra is the sixth in line, representing harmony. A relationship should be built on harmony, otherwise it cannot last long. To unblock that chakra, you must burn Ajna incense and essential oils. Myrrh, nutmeg, and St. John's Wort are superb. Your affirmations should be all about awareness and trusting your intuition, opening your third eye. "I let my intuition guide me", "I trust in what I feel" and "My spiritual truth guides me" are all spot on. Dolphin, locust and child's pose will help you greatly in your goal to reach that higher level of awareness in yoga.

Finally, the crown. This chakra represents connection, which is the quintessence of a relationship. Stay connected and build a wall around you, so that you feel safe and intimate with each other. Burn Sahaswara incense and essential oils, such as frankincense, myrrh and camphor. Your affirmations here should be relevant to enlightenment and deep, spiritual connection with yourself and others. "I am guided from my higher, spiritual self", "I feel connected to the universe" and "I am an extension of the universe" are all great. Last but not least, in yoga you should select meditative postures, such as those of lotus, half lotus and the tree posture.

Now you know how to open your chakras and pursue your sexuality and creativity.

Useful Exercises to Add to Your Morning Ritual

Your body is sacred. It needs to be honored and respected at the deepest level. Don't let anyone tell you otherwise. If you want to elevate your sexuality and enjoy the benefits of seduction, you can do that through specific exercises. In fact, you can add those exercises to your morning ritual and resort to them, whenever you are in need of guidance.

- An interesting thing that you can do to ignite that sexual energy within your body is to get a diary or a blank piece of paper and write down the word "Seductress". This is what you are trying to unlock, after all, your inner seductress, which magnetizes others and makes you feel unstoppable. Then, after that you can start writing down words that you find relevant to the "Seductress". What connotations does that word bring to you? Do that and you will see that the spark will be fuelled. You will get these words and embody them, rather than just have them in your mind. They will be released and you will have the chance to skyrocket your sexuality.

- Sensuality can be boosted through another helpful exercise. You sit down cross legged and you start breathing slowly. Inhale and exhale without haste. Then you can move in a clockwork direction, breathing in as you move inward and breathing out as you move outward. After you have felt that sensual energy working for you, do the reverse. This movement will create sexual energy. As soon as we realize we have created enough energy to serve our purpose, we allow ourselves to feel it. Again, cross legged we slide our upper body to the front and then to the back, without moving our pelvis. Finally, we breathe deeply as we attempt to experience the energy we have created.

- Pelvic floor exercise is another wonderful option that boosts your sexuality and creativity. You lay down on the floor, making sure you have a rug or a mat below you. A pillow can be placed right below your thighs or underneath your knees. Open your hands, get your feet stepping on the ground, knees folded. You must ground your body now. Start with the shoulders, paying attention to your breathing at the same time. Lower the shoulders a tiny bit, and continue on with the spine. Feel it lengthen, sinking in underneath the surface. Then move forward with your hips and thighs, calves and heels. First focus on the right side and then the left one. Following that, feel the light shining all over your body and direct the light beams to your pelvic area. As you inhale, the light sinks deeper and moves closer to your pelvis. Squeeze and release power. Now think of this. The light you have felt within your pelvis becomes a bloomed rose. What do you do? You sit comfortably, allowing more space for the flower. Slowly, take deep breaths and repeat this expansive movement. When you feel complete, return to your initial position and experience that precious relaxation.

7

EMBRACING YOUR FEMININITY

I n this chapter I am going to focus on femininity as a virtue, urging you to embrace it and be proud of who you are. I am guessing by now that you have realized what femininity is all about. You are seeking to find ways to release femininity to the world. Your coming out of the closet as a true feminine might fill you with fear and anxiety. Modern society is not exactly keen on women who have embraced their feminine style. On the contrary, there are often references to women that make them seem like caricatures; many are ridiculed for what they do in their life. Too many stereotypes have developed over the years. A feminine woman dresses in pink, is somewhat silly or superficial, does not have physical power, and relies on the masculine for help.

However, femininity is so much more than that. You should not be afraid to show off your feminine side. Instead, you should embrace it, because it is your superpower. Without it, you would be ordinary and blunt. Thanks to femininity, you are elegant and stylish, you are sensitive and caring, you are smart and full of confidence, hopes and dreams, you are wonderful. Unless you stop relying on what other people think, you can never expect to free your mind and release your true power into the world. Believe it, now that your awakening is taking place, you can really thrive and enjoy your life more.

Your feminine energy determines a lot about yourself. If you enjoy being a woman, then there is no reason to withhold that pleasure. It is your right to shape your personality the way you like. Why would you ever suppress your real feelings? There is no reason to feel guilt or shame due to the long lasting discriminations we have suffered from. Times have changed and this is our moment. No matter how severely you have been traumatized, no matter how much shame you have felt in the past, this is the time to let go and believe in your unique feminine energy. Dare to be feminine, despite what others might say. Who cares, really?

I understand that some women may reject femininity, due to a traumatic situation they have experienced in the past. This is a defensive mechanism and you should not depend on that. Do not waste your life, settling for something that makes you feel less happy than you would be feeling through the release of your feminine energy. Masculine characteristics are typically considered better, in terms of safety and tradition. Most people would prefer them over the more sensitive feminine traits.

In order for you to embrace your femininity, you must first realize where it stems from. To do that, you will need some questions to be answered. So take a moment and think of the answers to the following: "Do you enjoy being a woman?", "What part of femininity do you like and what part makes you feel bad?", "When did you start thinking of femininity?", "Where do you want to be in five years' time?", "Who showed you to be feminine?" and "Are you truly feminine?" are great questions to spark that inner conversation with yourself. It is important to acknowledge your femininity and she when it is lacking. You will find that you are biased against femininity to an extent, due to society's depictions of and discrimination against women.

Now that you have a clearer picture of what femininity actually is, why don't you focus on who has influenced you towards forming your opinion on femininity? If you are afraid of embracing femininity, then probably someone has contributed to your view. It is possible that you have experienced discrimination in the family or at school or by your peers. Things get worse when the people we look up to the most turn out to be judgmental. In this way, we often change our point of view and suppress our own beliefs, so as to keep them pleased and satisfied.

Even in the case of trauma, you can reframe your femininity. This happens through a process you can do on your own. I know that you have been hurt, due to the fact we live in a patriarchal society. Nevertheless, there are aspects of femininity that you are still drawn to. There are details which make you want to be feminine. Find out which qualities are and stick to them. Being a feminine is not just being girly. You are creative and beautiful, you are nurturing and caring.

Women have all of these impressive qualities, making them divine. We are truly unique in the world. Ever since mankind came to exist, women thrived and were worshiped for their qualities. They were worshiped for everything they represented. Their connection to divinity, their healing powers, their compassion and their insight, their empathy and intuition, their wisdom and affection, these were elements that raised women to the pedestal they belonged to. However, things were bound to change. Men were threatened by the dominance of women. They felt lesser and lesser every day, and they could not stand that. This has been the driving force behind the establishment of patriarchy. Through accusations, false interpretations, sabotage, and confrontation, men took over power.

A lot of time has passed since the time period in which patriarchy became the norm in societies across the globe. Women were forced to compromise for less, until they started claiming more. This happened through feminism. This movement rocked the foundations of modern societies and brought huge changes in the way both sexes interact. Nonetheless, there is a major difference we cannot ignore. Through feminism, what women claimed and received was relevant to masculine traits, not feminine ones. Women were eager to live their lives as men, which they have pretty much accomplished so far. But has it been for their own good? I wouldn't think so! Women wanted to imitate masculine behavior, although their purpose is entirely different. We are entirely different. In fact, we complement men, we don't antagonize them and we don't want to be them. Both the feminine and masculine values are beautiful, so we should not abolish either.

You have come to terms with femininity and you are looking forward to implementing it into your daily life. There are millions of ways for you to do that. Pick the ones you really enjoy and go for it. Start paying attention to what you are wearing, so that each outfit represents who you are in a feminine way. Then, you can redecorate your home or just your personal space. You can reorganize the kitchen or change your haircut, dye your hair or start polishing your nails. Tiny details can work wonders towards changing the way you feel inside, as well as the way you look and radiate.

DRIVING MEN WILD

Do you enjoy being a woman? Then your feminine side is celebrated and cherished. This is good. You should know that expressing your feminine energy drives men wild! There are many things that you can do, so as to skyrocket their libido and make them want you like crazy. The best part is that you don't have to pretend. You simply let go of your sensuality and adjust your behavior slightly, in order to appeal to them more than they have ever imagined. Let's have a closer look at some useful tips, which will allow you to get your man thinking of nobody else but you, 24/7.

First and foremost, you need to be comfortable in your femininity. Slow down your breathing, be soft and warm. There is no point in dressing sexy, if you cannot support that without feeling awkward. You are meant to do things you like, not things that others find attractive. Nobody should suppress you and that includes yourself. Instead, make sure that you are comfortable in elegant outfits, pay attention to your hair and makeup, do things that boost your confidence and self esteem. In this way, not only will you look great, but you will also feel like a million dollars.

Next, you should be able to say "no". In the beginning, you might feel bad about turning down a suggestion or sticking to your own plans, rather than adjusting to your partner's routine. However, think of it a little differently. As a woman, you may have thought that you ought to be submissive. This is not the case! You have your own life. You are empowered and independent. So you can have your own interests, your likes and dislikes. If you are too tired to go out tonight, then you should stay home and take a long bath. Don't push yourself to the limits, simply because you want to please your man. He will understand that. In fact, he will be delighted to see that you don't depend on him. The odds are that you will make him want you even more, after having refused a couple of times to go out.

Similar to the above tip, you can make a few compromises, but only after letting him know about them. For instance, you can try out Mexican food, even if you have never thought about doing that due to the spices. "Normally, I would never go to a Mexican restaurant, but I am going to make an exception for you." seems like a great compliment to him. "I usually prefer hiking, but sure, we can go mountain biking if you want. I can try this!", "Hm, I always get a martini, but now I will try what you are having for the first time." are just a few of the ways in which you can make him feel special. Since he is making you experiment with something different for the first time, he is extraordinary, right?

Next thing you can do is to allow your man to do something for you. I know this sounds almost like nothing you have ever been taught in life. Us women have learned the hard way to be strong and independent, expressing our masculine energy whenever possible. Nevertheless, you need to twist that a little, just as a reminder that you are feminine and you are in need of protection. There is nothing wrong in appearing vulnerable at times. Of course, you should not go to extremes and come across as helpless. Just a tiny bit. "Oh how thoughtful of you to cook dinner, I am too tired to cook for myself and

I am famished!", "Thank you for buying the groceries because I forgot about it" are wonderful ways to let him know he is needed.

The key component to making your man want you beyond comparison is to give him space and time. You know, we tend to react differently to men and this has its roots to science. Men don't process cortisol hormone like women, which makes them more prone to bursting with emotions. This is why men are more likely to snap and lose control. When you think of the way your man responds to you, it is really important that you take this into account. Otherwise, you will feel like he is not treating you right. So if you are willing to let that steam off and allow your man some breathing space, he will appreciate it a great deal. He will see that you are getting him, which will make him get closer to you eventually.

You should never rely on a man for your happiness. This is totally independent, since you can be happy on your own. Attracting a man should be all about fun, and it should be a part of your divine self expression. Always keep that in mind and be generous with your divine feminine energy, letting your man see what lies beneath the surface and introducing him to the wonders lying ahead. He will be crazy about you in no time!

Sexual Energy Activation and Nurturing

Your sexual energy should be celebrated, because you are entitled to absolute passion and pleasure. Why would you want to suppress your needs? Your sensuality will guide you to the highest levels of awareness, offering you the opportunity to enjoy life like you have never before. So you must find ways to activate and nurture your sexual energy, so that it grows and expands from within. There are many things you can do, as long as you realize that the energy should be contained within you to give its maximum potential.

First off, we start with food. Yes, whatever we eat affects us in more ways than we can imagine. This means that you need to pay attention to what you eat, not only to maintain your ideal weight and remain healthy. Each food you choose will influence the quality of your sexual energy. Feel free to eat fresh vegetables and fruit as much as possible, ensuring that you get most of that food raw. Avoid processed foods, artificial sweeteners and colorings, heavy cream, and too much fat.

Instead, appreciate flavor and texture. Choose quality over quantity and make every bite count. As for liquids, drink a lot of water and indulge in green and herbal tea, as well as moscato wine several times a day. This will bring you closer to divinity, so see if you enjoy the taste. I am sure you will!

Then, pamper yourself as much as you can. Have a long bath with salts and essential oils, clearing your mind from anything unnecessary. Get rid of the tension with a nice massage, meditate or engage in yoga sessions. Go out for a walk, take in the fresh air, and feel the calmness surrounding you. Take some time off, dedicate it to yourself and make the most of every moment. We have been used to squeezing in as many things as we can within the day. However, this only fills us with anxiety and we are always left feeling incomplete. At the end of the day, what matters is that we have pleased ourselves, we have done our best, and we have connected to the ones we love.

Have you ever tried mystical dance? This is the best way to dance from within you, so that you awaken the divine feminine energy. You need to understand the chakras of your body and release the tension, expanding the energy. Belly dance is an excellent form of mystical dance, so you can try it out and see what it brings out to you. The three steps to truly embrace your sexual energy and express it to the world include ways to relax, ignite the energy, and then contain it. So after having relaxed through deep breathing techniques, meditation and positive affirmations, you can ignite the energy through belly dance. Starting from the backbone and the first chakra, you can communicate with the universe through your body. Feel the energy expanding and moving upward, but keep it contained. This will help you experience energy at its fullest potential, without dispersing it into the world. Keep it within you, treasure it and enjoy.

Once you have done that, you will feel empowered and ready to take on the world. No more boundaries holding you back from enjoyment, no more taboos to overcome. You deserve to experience the full magnitude of pleasure deriving from your sexual energy, in alignment with the universe.

Antagonizing Men: Is This Real?

As I pointed out earlier in the book, there is absolutely no reason why you should antagonize men and compare yourself to them. In fact, if there is one thing we have learned so far about human relationships, it is the acknowledgement that both men and women should create the perfect balance to thrive together. Just like Yin and Yang, you need to find the right proportions to accomplish the ideal unity. Yin energy can be found in the calmness of subtle colors and soft music, and in the relaxation derived from the water gently flowing into the sea. On the other hand, there is Yang energy, which is far more active and can be seen in more intense light, colors and sounds. There is no comparison between the two energies, only an effort to balance and create something beautiful in the world.

Women have been misled to believe that they need to antagonize men, trying to outrank them, and reclaim what they have lost. This is a vicious cycle, since it strips women of their uniqueness and shows no actual desire to find harmony in life. A woman should not look at men and try to be more like them. Obviously, as discussed before, there are masculine aspects and characteristics in each individual, including women. However, this does not mean that a woman ought to change her very essence and let those masculine traits prevail. In this way, she will lose the divine feminine energy, which is vital for her well being and the celebration of her identity.

When a man and a woman are joined together, a true miracle takes place. There are forces so different, yet complementing one another. You don't need to do your best, in pursuit of proving that you are better than men. This is not a race, nor a competition. Nevertheless, you should stand your ground and claim what you want. You have the power to lay the foundations for a fruitful relationship, which is based on mutual understanding, love, and affection. Do not try to spoil that, by proving your point or sticking to feelings of revenge and spite. This is not who you are. Your union should be a blessing, rather than a constant conflict. Remember the Law of Polarity (Create Balance And Harmony Using the Law of Polarity, 2016). According to this acknowledgement, for every action there is an equal reaction of the same size and intensity. Everything in life comes with two poles, for example, good and evil. Everything is in fact dual in life. This means that we people are in search of our second pole to feel whole again. What we manifest is a combination of the two poles, trying to acquire balance. You should not forget that.

Men are not the enemy here. If anything, they should be our allies. We are in this together. They are as lost as we are, in the journey towards enlightenment and personal awareness. We dive deep inside and we try to explore the unknown. Both men and women seek harmony in a relationship. It is only fair to assume that this harmony can be reached through profound understanding, as well as the realization that we are not the same. We are equal, but not the same. Nobody is superior; instead, our value is identical. This is how we are meant to structure a solid relationship, which is going to make the relationship last, despite the toll of time.

❦ 8 ❦

RELEASE PAST TRAUMA AND MAKE SPACE FOR YOUR DIVINE FEMININE AWAKENING

E ver since you were a little girl, you were told to change the way that you behaved. At the same time, any sign of femininity that you showed seems to have triggered negative reactions. Does that sound familiar? When you are not certain of yourself and your identity, you grow up questioning everything. You question your power and your personal value, you doubt whether you are worthy enough to trigger love and pleasure, you shy away from anything that makes you feel and look womanly. But is this really the way to be? Do you truly want to compromise everything, just to fit in the generic boxes others have created for you?

It feels wrong to live your life according to what others dictate. Especially when your life is so unique and you are able to experience greatness and divinity. First, you need to clear out trauma from your past, shifting your mindset and resetting your life. You must delve into deep research and unlearn what you have been taught all these years. It requires a lot of effort and hard work, but I promise it is worth it. What you need to do is to unearth and ground yourself in your truth. It is what you believe and what you want that matters the most.

You have been wounded deeply, your feminine side has been traumatized and now you are experiencing the side effects of this trauma. Maybe your sexual identity has become a matter of criticism, a reason to feel ashamed. Everyone around you has been looking at you like you are nothing but a vessel of sexual pleasure. Your figure triggers desires and this is perfectly OK for men. They can express that desire, without paying attention to your emotions. Whether you feel comfortable or not, they can comment on the way you look, and they can make their move, even if it causes you distress.

On the other hand, you are always advised to be solemn and subtle. You should not be aggressive or provoke men, because then you will have it coming. In society, a woman who is liberated and expresses her femininity is almost always considered provocative. She should slow down, cover her true self, and settle for society's standards as to what is acceptable and what isn't. This can lead to a hyper sense of sexuality. So instead of feeling comfortable and fine being sexy, you use that to manipulate others. You know that this is a tool, an advantage you have over men. Why not use it to your benefit? More than that, you seduce and control men with the most powerful thing on you—because this is what you have been taught to believe.

The other way in which trauma can appear in your life is through suppressed emotions. To be more specific, you have always heard others telling you to be tough. Us women are often characterized as too soft, powerless, and unable to control our emotions. It is absolutely understandable why women are more sensitive. It is in their feminine side of existence. However, society does not have room for that. On the contrary, women are expected to toughen up and endure hardships, as well as negative feelings, without complaining. It is a cruel world, but you need to pull through and find ways to cope with that. Moreover, we are told that we should be more like men. What does a man do when something bad comes along? He deals with it, no crying, no whining.

With that in mind, you learn how to suppress your emotions while you are growing up. You undervalue their meaning and you become accustomed to imitating masculine behavior. There is nothing wrong in having a masculine side. In fact, having the perfect balance between masculine and feminine would be the right way to live your life. But this doesn't mean that you should forget what it's like to be a woman. Showing compassion, being sensitive and open, warm and soft—these are all elements that define who you really are. These traits reveal your greatness and they should not be forgone.

UNBURDEN YOURSELF FROM HEAVY BAGGAGE

Unrooting past traumas to make space for your divine feminine awakening is of the essence. You need to be strong and take all the necessary steps so that you can move forward. When you have so much weight on your shoulders, it is only fair that you feel overwhelmed and exhausted. On the contrary, once you deal with the issues that have been troubling you and get your closure, you will feel lighter than ever before. So do not waste any more time. Find what is dragging you down and get rid of it at once. You ought to deal with these issues by clearing the subconscious beliefs that you have as a woman, and this book will not only help you become aware of your limiting beliefs, but also move through them. Healing the inner child can make space for your awakening.

The first thing you need to do is to confront the trauma. It is imperative that you address clearly what has traumatized you, because otherwise you cannot deal with it properly. When you are facing an unknown threat, there is no effective way to overcome the problem and move past it. So confrontation is the key to success. If you keep burying it underground, then you will only prolong a negative situation and prevent yourself from experiencing what you are entitled to. Do not hide yourself from the truth; do not conceal the facts or distort reality.

Next, you should talk about what happened. There is great flexibility in how to achieve that. Some people might choose therapy, because they feel like trusting a professional. Of course, this is a good thing. The experts will guide you through the process of analyzing the details regarding your trauma. Through proper questions, you will have the opportunity to read in between the lines and see exactly what has triggered your wound. Was it a specific incident or was it a person that made you feel bad? Alternatively, women can turn to their friends for releasing their tension and letting off some steam. Family can serve exactly the same way, although most people think family members may pressure trauma victims into not opening up. Last but not least, a journal can be quite liberating. So if you express yourself in writing, you can try out gathering your thoughts in a diary.

Moving forward, it is time to accept what has happened. This is the only way for you to find your peace. Although it can make you feel pain, you need to go through that pain to recover. You should be ready to accept that everything happens for a reason. Holding on to the past will destroy your life. It will be an anchor, which drives you to the bottom. You need to get rid of the anchor's chain, so as to emerge back on the surface. Use that trauma as a lesson and not as a pattern. Finally, you have completed the cycle and you are ready to move on. No more excuses, no more alibi for suffering. You are free.

Easy to Follow Morning Ritual

What do you do when you wake up in the morning? Are you one of these people, who sets a dozen alarms, only to click on the "snooze" button? This is only buying you a fraction of the time you should be sleeping, you know that, right? Or maybe you stand up right after the first alarm has rung, so as to get ready and head to work? Whatever you do, chances are that you do not devote much time to yourself. Too bad! Your soul needs nourishment, as much as your body does. Therefore, you need to take care of your mental clarity and your calmness. To do that, you will need to change some old vices of yours.

By shifting your habits, you will discover a whole new world. In this way, you will be able to experiment with new patterns that might become your favorite. First off, you must commit to waking up slightly earlier than what you would have hoped. This will allow you to wake up more naturally, avoiding tension and unnecessary stress. Then, you should prepare yourself a hearty and healthy breakfast. It is essential that you get hydrated, letting your body replenish all the valuable components it lost overnight. Find out which foods really agree with your digestive system, while at the same time offering you the nutrients and energy you need for a full day ahead.

Next, you must incorporate some sort of physical exercise in your morning ritual. Obviously, it is best that you practice meditation and special exercises, meant to trigger different parts of your body. However, you must also find the time to appreciate the moment and let go of the stress. This is the perfect way to start your day. Back to exercise, you should implement a daily feminine morning ritual that focuses on clearing trauma, limiting self beliefs, shame and realigning with your sacred feminine energy. There are quite a few different techniques and sets of exercises that you can try out. Below, you will find some really helpful and easy exercises which you can fit in your daily schedule. Start your day with this workout and you will feel refreshed, regenerated and filled with energy.

First off, we start with TRE exercises. TRE stands for Trauma Releasing Exercises. If you observe the animal kingdom, you will notice a lot of animals do that to shake off any tension. The same applies to humans, so you should really experiment with the power of shaking off the trauma from your body. One of the best exercises to do is to stand up and move your back towards the wall. Then you should slowly move your body downward, while making your legs create an angle and opening them slightly. So in the end, it will be like you are sitting on an invisible chair, supporting your body through the back and mainly through the legs. As soon as you feel that you are on the brink of collapsing due to the weight, you get a little higher and you continue working out like that. After having almost resumed your initial standing position, you will feel your muscles tremor. You must then lie down on your back, knees raised, with the bottom your feet planted firmly on the floor a few inches apart. Experiment with moving your knees apart to discover what creates the most intense shaking. This will release stored trauma in your body. I practice TRE at least 30 minutes a day and have felt huge results! To stay productive, I often read while shaking out.

If you want a different TRE exercise, then you can lay down and connect your feet, while bending your legs. Now your position will be like that of a frog. When you feel comfortable with that, try to raise your body towards the sky. This is an excellent exercise for toning up your muscles as well. While you are staying in that position, you will realize that the muscles are burning. Tighten up your buttocks, and feel the muscles getting strained. Repeat as many times as it takes, so as to promote the tremor. You will be impressed by the results. Once again, you must allow time to shake out in the lying position.

EFT exercises stand for Emotional Freedom Techniques. When you are feeling overwhelmed by stress or anxiety, depression or even chronic pain, this can work wonders for you. The whole concept is based on alternative medicine like acupuncture, neuro-linguistic programming, and a lot more. It would be great to add some EFT exercises in your morning ritual. This involves tapping specific parts of your body, while keeping a steady rhythm and repeating positive affirmations. In this case, you can start tapping the external part of your palm and then move on your face. The spot underneath your eyes, on your cheeks, right below your nose, on your chin, on your ribs and just below your armpits—these are all exceptional spots to practice EFT tapping. Type EFT tapping into YouTube and there are hundreds of results! I personally focus on one tapping video until I feel that issue resolve on my life. For example, if I am feeling shame during a particular week, I will focus primarily on a shame EFT tapping video that week, or until I have cleared it.

As for what you can say, try something similar to the following: "I have been through a lot of pressure. There is trauma in my life, which has messed with my entire being. I have been hurt, I have cried, and I have suffered enough. Now it is my time to shine. I am powerful enough to leave this trauma behind. It is within my power to fight back and overcome the hardship that has happened to me. I am strong and wonderful." This is just an example, so that you can experiment with what makes you feel better. Add positive affirmations, which will help you build on your confidence and see who you really are. You better believe it!

❧ 9 ❧

GRASP YOUR DIVINE FEMININE
AWAKENING

Nobody was born knowing all the answers to their questions. And there is one particular question which has been on your mind for quite some time now. Of course, this has been one of the main reasons why you have got your hands on this book. You are searching for the answers, which will enlighten you as to your journey towards divine feminine awakening. We are all humans and humans need answers. We are in need of positive feedback and confirmation that we are on the right path. However, there is not a clear "yes or no" verdict. You cannot visit a professional to get diagnosed as awakening or not, can you? So in moments of doubt, you must turn to whoever holds the wisdom and knowledge to guide you.

Are you wondering whether or not your divine feminine is finally awakening? There are times when we feel over the moon, only to find out that we have been deceived by the signs. Especially when it comes to discovering your divine power, the stakes are way too high. I understand that you are feeling anticipation to experience what is about to come. But is that truly happening? Are you indeed on your way to experience this wonderful feeling? Are you about to turn over a new leaf? I am going to offer you a plethora of signs, so that you know your imagination is not playing tricks on you. If you tick more than a few of

these boxes, then you are indeed waking up. So are you ready to identify hese tell tale signs?

Obviously, one of the fundamental signs that you are waking up is
your deepest intuition. You will feel it in your bones. You will be sure
that something is changing, just like a caterpillar which is about to turn
into a butterfly. This transformation is huge and will happen from
within. Have you ever felt certain about anything in your life? For
those of you who have felt so in love that anything else doesn't matter,
this will be quite similar. Have you ever met women who have decided
to change their life against all odds, because they felt right? Or maybe
you are one of these women? This is the feeling, so look out for that
sign as an amuse bouche, the perfect start to a delectable meal ahead!

ARE YOU WAKING UP FROM YOUR HIBERNATION?

Your feminine divine power is slowly waking up, so how can you
tell? One of the things that should alarm you is the fact that you are
always digging deeper, in pursuit of the real "you". It is a great thing to
try and figure out who you are, meaning that you don't know. This self
doubt reveals that you are much more than what you thought you
were. The more you discover about yourself, the more you get to love
your uniqueness. You cherish it and embrace it. There is nothing
better than knowing you don't fit any boxes, but you are extraordinary
and special.

At the same time, you get rid of selfishness. There is no "ego" in
the picture. As a Starseed, you have been incarnated in this life to lay
the world a helping hand. You are meant to offer, rather than act on
egoism and personal interests. This doesn't mean that you forget to

love yourself—not at all. One of the signs that you are on your way to your awakening is the fact that you take great care of yourself. Who is more precious than you, after all? As a matter of fact, you will be prone to improving your diet and making some radical changes about your wellness. For instance, you will want to quit smoking or give up on sugar, coffee or fat altogether.

Moving on with the signs that should alert you you are on the route to success, you will notice a significant shift in the way you treat others. Until now you have been accustomed to bending the knee, whenever there was a conflict. You pretty much did what others expected of you. It feels like you didn't have your own will. But now, you feel it in your gut that something has changed. Now you don't worry about what others might say. The protagonist in your own movie is you and you alone. What is more, you no longer succumb to patriarchal concepts. Even if you have learned all your life to follow these rules, they no longer speak to you. You know better than that.

As we discussed earlier in the book, you leave all those bitter experiences in the past. You don't hold grudges, nor do you fall back into the same traps. This is the past; what is done is done. Now a potential setback cannot be used as an excuse to shape the future in a negative pattern. So you let go of all the worrisome experiences, all the mistakes and all the misconceptions. Of course, this doesn't mean that you should beat yourself up. Contrary to what you may think, one of the signs has to do with compassion towards yourself and forgiveness. You have done nothing wrong, after all. Life does not come with its own manual, so trial and error is totally allowed.

Well, you should be prepared for all these good things coming your way, letting you in on the secret you are finally waking up. Nevertheless, it is not all roses and sunshine. This is an enormous shift in your life, which will definitely make you feel scared. You will be frightened at the thought that nothing should be taken for granted. On the contrary, you must always be ready to doubt even the very core of your existence. Is everything you have lived so far a lie? This can bring you down, causing depression and even suicidal thoughts. Please be patient, you will get through this. It is meant to be an extraordinary experience, which only a few are ever going to enjoy in life. Don't feel helpless, as you are nothing like that.

It makes sense that you will feel the need to share your experience with others. Being awakened and knowing it takes a lot of courage. In order to deal with the changes that happen all the time, you should find your community. Hence, you will feel the urge to find your peers. You will want to explore the places, where you can meet like minded people to talk about everything you have been experiencing. There is nothing alarming about that. In fact, we all require support at times. On the bright side, despite what you may initially think, you will eventually restore your hope. Besides, you have been blessed and this is something to celebrate, rather than frown upon.

Over time, the signs you see become clearer and clearer. Your confidence strengthens, as you are beginning to realize what is truly taking place. It is not rare for people like you to have breakthroughs and epiphanies. Things will start making sense, as you are connecting all the dots. You will soon feel more powerful than ever, certain about where you are heading. Although self-hatred could have crept in, filling you with disappointment, you loathe yourself no more. How could you? You are sacred, believe in that. Your ego is transformed, your chakras are unblocked, and you feel ready for your new life.

Way to Go, Girl!

If you have made it that far, you most likely have experienced those early awakening signs in your life, so congratulations! This is an amazing journey, which has just begun. Take a moment and sink it in, trying to fully perceive what is going on. You are the chosen, you are sacred, you are unique. No one is going to take that power away from you, because you won't let them. You are in control of your emotions, you are in control of your entity. Imagine the full potential of releasing your divine feminine energy into the world. Let it flow right through you and feel what it can do. You are divine and no one can take that away from you. Your power has been there all along, but you have not been able to see that. Now you know and it is only fair that you change your life, based on your recent revelations.

Your instinct was right. That voice in your head, which kept telling you not to give up, is now shouting out with joy and excitement. This is your moment, girl. You ought to be proud of yourself. You have come this far, interpreting the signs and pursuing your dreams and hopes. Some people would say you were overly enthusiastic, some others would call you crazy. Doubting others and making them feel bad is something most people resort to when they feel threatened. And being different always poses a threat to others. But this doesn't mean you should look forward to uniformity. You did not give in to the temptation to please others by changing your personality. What you did took courage, and you lived up to the expectations.

It has been a rocky road, for sure. I imagine that most people were not there by your side. During your explorations, many of your so-called friends and family did nothing but judge you. They have been questioning your motives and they have been looking down on you ever since you have expressed your need to delve into this soul-searching experience. Many people find it hard to get rid of their old beliefs. They stick to what they know and they are inflexible, leaving no room for the tiniest bit of change. These are the first to doubt you, even when you have evidence to back up your claims.

Through the hardships, you managed to rise from the ashes like the phoenix. You have persisted in your goals and found what you were looking for. All these people who did not hesitate to call you names and shame you, make fun of you or even isolate you socially—where are they now? Are they close to you, so as to witness your transformation? I certainly hope they get to see what has become of you. It is going to be a memorable day, when you feel indifferent toward their attitudes and actions. Just remember, your divinity is unquestionable. You are sacred and nobody should tell you otherwise.

Your efforts have undoubtedly persevered through hardship. All these results have come through sweat and tears. This only makes your victory sweeter. You know that you have persisted in your goals, even when everyone around you told you to quit. Not only did you not listen to their advice, but you pushed yourself to experience your awakening and enjoy what lies ahead. It is a wonder that you survived, a wonder that you have orchestrated on your own. You deserve congratulations, as a way to express my gratitude for not giving up. Us women must empower one another and help each other to overcome any shadows or low points during this demanding process. Congratulations for what you have achieved thus far, we are all looking forward to what comes up next.

There is greatness ahead for you, dear. The road will not be paved with roses, but you have been forged with fire and steel. You can take on any challenge that comes your way. Now, one final sign to look for. I am sure it is already there. Your third eye is open, isn't it? Focus and see right through, see what it unveils for you. Exciting times, truly exciting times ahead...

❧ 10 ❧

GUIDED MEDITATIONS TO TAKE
YOU BY THE HAND

There are several guided meditations that you can do to experience your divine awakening, and they will make the difference in your life. Among them, feel free to find the meditations that actually speak to you. The feminine energy awakening guided meditation is the first meditation which we are going to focus on in this section. It allows you to empower yourself and become the woman you have always dreamed of being.

You start by sitting comfortably on the floor, using a blanket or a soft mat. You stretch a little, making sure that all your muscles are relaxed. You place your palms in your lap. Focus on your breath, noticing how the air flows inside and then outside. Now it is time to focus on connecting with your inner feminine energy. Begin to become aware of a pink rose, which is blooming inside your heart. Pay attention to each petal, watching as the rose begins to grow and expand. The rose is getting bigger and wider with your every breath. Now your awareness should be on the top of your head, and you may be experiencing a slight tingling sensation.

As you are watching this, soft pink light illuminates you. It bathes you from the top of your head all the way down to your hips and legs. This is all you see, pink light that symbolizes pure love. This is awakening your feminine energy. You bring light into your darkness, as the Goddess within you guides you without judgment. Slowly, you are starting to come to terms with unconditional acceptance. Notice her powerful presence washing over you. The powerful feminine energy is awakening, feeling the change in your physical body, your mind and your heart. This is a transformation that you welcome.

Picture yourself on top of the mountain, with the air blowing softly, and touching your cheeks, fondling your hair. Stay fully connected to your inner goddess, bringing this awareness back to where you are now. Open your eyes slowly, feeling the tips of your fingers and toes, lowering your shoulders. This is how you get closer to your feminine energy, awakening it to enjoy the maximum benefits that can be derived from this unpretentious flow.

BALANCING MASCULINE AND FEMININE ENERGIES GUIDED MEDITATION

Through the balancing masculine and feminine energies guided meditation, you will be able to reach out to your oneness and experience completion, absolute balance and a sense of pure wellbeing. This is a marvelous way to get closer to both your sides, stop fighting one another and enjoy the best of the masculine, and the feminine, sides within you.

You sit comfortably somewhere and start to breathe in and out, really gently and slowly. Let go of your worries and everything that has been troubling you. Close your eyes and go to a peaceful place, travel somewhere you feel comfortable and set out on your new journey. This can be a familiar place, or a place you have never seen before in your life. Let the colors embrace you, soothing your soul. What colors surround you? See yourself, as you are glowing with an immense light. You are radiant. Notice all the details about yourself. Are you small or big, are you beautiful, radiant, elegant? Take a moment and concentrate on your chakras. Which of those chakras are already glowing in your body? All your different energy centers should start glowing, so pay attention to those that are not quite there yet.

Now, look in the distance. There is another being coming towards you, a being of the opposite sex in a radiant form. As the being gets closer and closer, you realize that you are equally beautiful, equally radiant, equally sized. You are the exact opposite polarity, but everything else is similar. Greet that being with your palms, approaching even more. Your palms touch and then slowly you begin merging. As you are becoming one, you feel that energy igniting you. There is an awakening of the opposite traits, the opposite energy within you. Your masculine energy is spiked and complements your feminine traits. Doesn't it feel wonderful?

The presence of this other being ignites the central column of your body, which offers you the chance to experience the absolute balance between your masculine and feminine energies. The union of these two distinct energies connects you to that higher power. Finally, it is time for that being to flow out of your body and leave. This allows you to remain who you are. However, you have the opportunity to merge whenever you feel like doing so. You can come to this place in your mind anytime and experience the same thing. To regain consciousness and wake up, start breathing deeply, and move your toes and fingers slightly.

Reiki Goddess Guided Meditation

If you are having trouble sleeping, or if you are overly stressed, and you want to release the tension, the Reiki Goddess guided meditation is a superb option for you.

Close your eyes and breathe deeply. Let go, as you set out on a journey to the most powerful landscapes. In fact, you are floating and you can feel your feet slowly ascending to the skies. There, you find the Goddess. As you are exhaling, you free your mind and think of a tale about time. Time started giving orders to the planets, the solar system, the different galaxies, as Hope breathed life into them. The Temptress instilled her blessings and curiosity started sinking in, so Time moved faster and faster. More and more stars were added to the night sky, offering their immense glow to the universe. Then, Time moved even faster and colors spread all over the world. Thousands of chromatic shades, lovely hues in perfect harmony, creating master-pieces of nature.

Time could not stand still, so every heartbeat sounded like music and motivated time to move faster and faster. As Time wandered through the universe, it stumbled upon a Sun. The Sun had no beat, unlike everything else in the world. So it had no knowledge of its birth, no curiosity to find out, no blessing whatsoever. With the Sun shining brightly and giving its warmth to the universe, Time had to slow down. Time could not even move, so he literally contained himself while trying to move round the Sun. Now Time was yearning for love, but love was nowhere to be found. He could not join the rest of the universe, listen to the beat, and feel the curiosity necessary for him to continue on hus trajectory.

In response to Time's yearning, the universe created the Goddess of Love. She came to Time's rescue and sat on his left shoulder. So, having Time by her side, the Goddess of Love began teaching the Sun. She sang sweetly, while butterflies filled her hands, and bee honey aromas filled the atmosphere. Her voice and singing was healing. The Goddess then took the Sun and neatly placed everything in the universe just so to bring all into balance. The planets, the moons, the shooting stars, the suns, and everything was in perfect sync to produce the most magnificent outcome.

The Goddess of Love talked to the Sun, explaining that there is a special beat within each and every single one of us. If you truly listen, you will be able to hear that special tune, the beat that keeps us in harmony with the rest of the universe. This beat comes in the form of the heart.

Feminine Inner Child Healing Guided Meditation

Your family raised you in a certain way, often going above and beyond to do what is right. They protected and cherished you, they nourished and provided for you. However, this doesn't mean that you are left unwounded by the process of growing up. There are traumas that lie there beneath the surface and hold you back from enjoying life to the fullest. When you indulge in the inner child healing meditation, it will help you to ease and resolve past traumas. Let us see how you can practice this meditation.

You begin by closing your eyes. You take a deep, calm breath. Slow down, unwind and relax. Lower your shoulders a bit, let them fall a little bit. Your entire body falls lower. Then you start thinking of your past, your life as a child. You visualize it and think of all the negativity, all the bad situations that have brought you to where you are now, traumatized and helpless. You should have found protection and reassurance, but you didn't. Next, visualize your life's timeline. There is a light at the end of the timeline, and you are getting closer to it. With every breath you take, feel the light surrounding you, warming you, illuminating every cell of your body.

Imagine that the vortexes on the bottom of your feet open so that they receive the same light from mother earth. Now you feel lighter and healthier than ever, it is time to look back to the dysfunctional behavior that led to your trauma. Try to identify where it began. Keep your eyes closed, feeling the warm energy overwhelming you. You are ready to travel back to your childhood. Once you locate that very moment, open the door right in front of you. What you find there is amazing. There is your figure, as well as the figure of yourself as a child.

Observe each other and, when you feel comfortable enough, start talking to your younger self. It is going to be emotional, for sure. Try to reassure the child that everything will be alright. You are the living and breathing manifestation that everything will work out in the end. Take the child in your arms, comfort her, and let her know that you are sorry you couldn't be there for her. Allow dialog between the two. This child is sweet and innocent. Take a few moments, comfort her, and make her feel secure. Notice how innocent and hopeful she is, all she needs is love. Unfortunately, parents or caregivers could not provide that and so the child was programmed in the wrong way.

Then, go ahead and talk to the child. "Sweet little child, I love you. I support you. You are wonderful and you can do anything you set your mind on. I will keep you safe and protected from all harm" Say all the things that you have been longing to hear and no one has ever told you. This will correct the programming for this child. Let them know the negative consequences of their unhealthy patterns. "Sweet child, don't take care of your parents. It is not meant to be this way. Do not listen to what others say. You are kind and worthy, you deserve to be loved. You deserve to be happy. Others projected their fears, their wounds and their problems onto you, and they weren't yours to take. Instead, take care of yourself and yourself, alone."

In the end, you should invite your younger version to come with you, so that you can keep them safe like you promised. Allow the child to climb up and come with you, merging within your current figure. Then, take a few calming, deep breaths, and feel the purifying light within you. Now you can bring forward your past self to your current state, you can erase all the traumas and correct the dysfunctions that have occurred from your childhood. Relax, sigh with relief, and appreciate the moment. You are ready to come back. Feel your toes wiggle and open your eyes. Stretch a little and smile. You have made it to the finish line.

MANIFESTING YOUR BEAUTIFUL LIFE WITH YOUR DIVINE FEMININE ENERGY

E xperiencing your divine feminine energy, don't you feel that something has changed in your life? I am not referring to the theoretical changes, but to what happens in your everyday life. After having reached that point where you don't doubt your divinity anymore, a whole new world of potential unfolds. This is where you truly grasp what has happened. Your life will never be the same. What you have been dreaming of all this time, what you have been secretly wishing to happen, is here. What does this mean for you, practically speaking?

There are many things in life that cause anxiety and stress, keeping you from truly appreciating the moment and enjoying your life 100%. Most people stress over money, health and relationships, as well as professional issues. It is in your hands to pick out what is troubling you more in your life, so as to change it according to your desires. You are holding the power required to attract what you are lacking. If you are wondering how you can achieve that, it is quite simple and straightforward. You will need the power of your mind to succeed in flipping your life upside down. Have you ever spent time alone, envisioning how you would have wanted your life to be? There are times when people feel down and they are trying to hold on to something; a memory, a person, a dream. So they often end up fantasizing about their dream life. They imagine how the perfect house would be, along with the perfect partner and the perfect career. Of course, all that comes with a generous amount of money in their bank account. This is by far the best company!

By reaching deep into your divine feminine energy and using it to your benefit, you can create the basis on which to live your dream life. Even if this sounds too good to be true, indeed you can shape your future with the power of your inner goddess. Think carefully and imagine what would make you happy. Then, ask the universe to provide that for you—just wait and see. Before you know it, your entire life will have changed its course. You will be en route to success, any way you define the term. If you ask from your inner goddess to bring you wealth, then you should expect riches to come your way, even without you knowing it. If, however, you have asked for health and wellness, you will feel empowered to improve your diet and work-out. You will feel more motivated than ever to stick to your plan, so that you become the healthiest, fittest, happiest version of yourself.

There is nothing stopping you, now that you know the secret. Your divine feminine energy is powerful enough to cause chaos. Of course, this is not what you want. On the contrary, what you are seeking is all about finding harmony and the perfect balance in life. Whatever makes you happy should be given to you in a heartbeat. There is no need to wait and rely on luck. Let us face the truth, luck always favors the bold and daring in life. You should do your part, rather than expect others to come to your rescue. With your inner goddess, there is nobody else you need.

LAW OF ATTRACTION AND FEMININE ENERGY

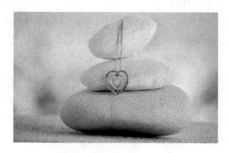

"When you want something, all the universe conspires in helping you to achieve it" (Paulo Coelho - Wikiquote, n.d.) This is a famous quote from Paulo Coelho, which pretty much sums up what Law of Attraction is. Let us have a look at how the Law of Attraction (The Law Of Attraction - Discover How to Improve Your Life, n.d.), this New Thought Philosophy, can work wonders on our life. Through the use of feminine energy, we can attract what we want and make the most of our desires. In this way, we can pursue wealth, abundance, love, career, and everything else our heart desires, if we use our divine energy properly.

First of all, take a moment and think about it. Have you ever been in a situation when wanting something actually causes you physical pain? Your heart just hurts, because you want something so much. If you have ever watched YouTube videos of children reacting to puppies and kittens, you will know what I mean. As soon as a parent offers the child a puppy, the child bursts out in tears. The emotions are overflowing, making the child unable to restrain themselves. The same happens when you cry joyous tears at the thought of a loved one or in anticipation of an important event. In a similar pattern, your over-desiring leads to self doubt and second guessing as to whether or not this is the right choice for you. Even though you might have spent a lot of time thinking of something, the moment you obtain it, you instantly start doubting that it was the best decision. Both these options mean that you want something more than you are able to allow it. Can you grasp that concept? When you want something in excess, then you end up working against yourself. This will come back like a boomerang and hit you in the face, if you don't pay attention to the signs.

The secret lies in harmony and balance. Without the right balance, you cannot find your inner peace. More than that, you cannot enjoy what you are meant to enjoy in life. Balance that out and then you will be able to pursue what you are craving. Don't get carried away by emotions; instead, set realistic goals and anticipations. Besides, Rome was not built in a day. What does that mean for you? Well, you will need to make peace with where you are right now in order to get to where you want to be. It takes time to reassess your current situation and see how you can improve your life, one step at a time. So it is imperative that you find the silver lining and identify the good things in your current state.

Moving forward, you should not neglect the whole ritual of visualizing what it would feel like to get what you want when it comes to love. As a result, you picture yourself as the receiver and you analyze all the emotions that are sparked by your accomplishments. If you do that frequently, you will get the chance to reap the benefits of your imagination. As you think about your feelings, something truly marvelous happens. You will radiate these feelings to attract the thing you want. It makes sense that your aura attracts those you want and repels those you loathe. If you stick to that plan, you will notice that the wrong people will fade away and the right people will come closer to you. I know that you may be skeptical, but give it a try.

Focus on the things that you think you are lacking. For example, if you are in a bad financial state, then visualize that you are wealthy. Think of your riches, lay down your money, and see how much you have got. Use positive affirmations to convince your mind that you are already wealthy. You own a yacht, you have jewelry and stocks in your safe deposit box, and your bank account has more money than you could ever need in your life. If, on the other hand, you are mostly yearning for love and you are alone, then try to repeat time and over again that you are worthy of love and that your dream partner is right there searching for you. Believe in your ability to attract love and enjoy a wonderful relationship with the man of your dreams. He will come knocking on your door before you know it!

Equally important is for you to address the signs that reveal that you are on the right track towards success. When you lose hope, it makes sense that you find something to lift you up and restore your faith in yourself. What a better way to achieve that than to collect all the evidence that proves that your actions have had a positive impact on you and the rest of the world. It is uplifting to have the proof required, so that you know you are doing great. If you are walking blindfolded, you will always doubt as to whether or not you are moving in the right direction. Once you open your eyes, you instantly get the reassurance that you have been wishing to receive.

When you are actively pursuing a man to indulge in a new relationship, the Law of Attraction can help you out a great deal. Obviously, you first need to make sure that the man you are interested in is actually on the same page as you. I am not talking about being in love with you, but it is only fair to pursue a man who is not married, heterosexual, and open to new acquaintances. Otherwise, your odds will naturally diminish and the law of attraction is not the one to blame here. Then, you should focus on the essence of the man. This means that you should identify what feelings he brings out in you. These feelings are what is driving you to want to be with him. If you are asking yourself why this is a crucial part of forming the relationship, review how the Law of Attraction works. You need to elicit these feelings to yourself first and then from a man.

As an exercise to practice the Law of Attraction and the impact it has on your feminine energy, every morning you can write down whatever you want to happen within your day. This can be as small as enjoying a hearty, delectable meal, or as big as winning the lottery. Some of the things that you include on the list may sound nearly impossible. The same goes for the man of your dreams. Write down if you want to meet him, where you want to see him and what you want him to do. Write everything in detail and put them in a list, so that the universe can provide. Even if at first this all comes across as wishful thinking, you will soon perceive its meaning and true value.

Rather than sitting idle and doing nothing, or wondering why your life has become so stale and bitter, you need to step up. Take action and claim what is yours from the universe. It is essential that you actively pursue your dreams and hopes. There is no one to play that role for you. It is in your power to shape your destiny, so go ahead and do what you have to do. Before asking to receive, be sure to get rid of all the clutter within your mind and soul. Cleanse the negative energy, because this is the only path towards achieving a deeper connection to your higher self. You do not need all this noise. What you do need is to have an active contribution to your evolution. You set your mind on something and you do whatever it takes, persuading the universe that you are entitled to it.

Feminine Energy Manifestation Guided Meditation

A guided meditation that you can use to manifest your feminine energy is the following, but feel free to experiment with similar words of appreciation towards the universe. You should be relaxed, preferably in a place with which you are familiar and comfortable in. Use sage to clear the space and promote your meditation. Light some candles and sit quietly. This is a sacred ceremony, offering you the opportunity to reach your highest self. "Dear universe, I am worthy of receiving what I want in life. I am ready to enjoy the manifestation of my feminine energy. I want to have my purest desires fulfilled right away because I deserve them. May I receive everything I want for the common good of all women. It is my right to enjoy life to the fullest so as to benefit the world through my exceptional lifestyle. My desires come in perfect alignment with nature. I want to remain in harmony with Gaia and this is how I am able to achieve that. I deserve to feel happy."

As you can imagine, it is vital that you remain calm throughout the meditation. You need to control your breathing and set the pace, so that you reach within your feminine energy and request what is yours. Close your eyes, make sure that your muscles are relaxed and dive into the subconscious. You are aiming at an endless flow of energy. Find the perfect way to listen to your body and realize where that flow is directed. Keep your sense of calmness as you repeat the above positive affirmations. Feel the energy awakening and all those desires of yours slowly manifested before your eyes.

It all has to do with your beliefs. You need to be sure that you deserve what you are asking to manifest through your feminine energy. Unless you are confident that you are entitled to these claims, you will never manage to obtain them. It doesn't matter if you have spent all this time trying to shift your mindset. You ought to come across as super confident, absolutely certain of what you should enjoy in your life. This guided meditation is just giving you the vessel through which to express your inner thoughts.

This Is A Marathon, Not A Sprint

All this knowledge might make you want to dive right in and experience your true divine power to its full potential. However, this is not the best way to go. I understand why you are so excited, but you need to take it easy. There is so much more to master before you experiment with the impact of your divinity. You are so new to this that it is prudent to take a deep breath and remain calm. Let the universe work its magic, and you sit there relax and enjoy what comes next.

There is no shortcut to anywhere worth going, right? This is a wonderful thing to keep in mind the next time you are tempted to rush and push things. Instead, you need to practice the art of patience. It can be hard at times, but as soon as you have seen the benefits it offers, you will be grateful that you have taken things slowly. In the meantime, appreciate the moment and evaluate your progress. Track down all the changes that have taken place so far. Be appreciative of all the good things that have come your way. Cherish the special moments that you have experienced so far and get ready for the future thrills.

Think of where you were when you started this journey, and take a look at where you are now. You have managed to do all these amazing things, you have set the foundations for an even greater future life. You are now ready to reap the benefits of your choices. Nevertheless, change doesn't happen overnight and this is something you must come to terms with. There are several stages you should go through, before getting accustomed to that overwhelming power from within. You should tame this power and learn how to be in control. It takes time and real struggle to get there. So plan ahead, lay out your weapons, and structure a strategy that will pay off eventually.

You need to master the skills that you are beginning to obtain, and this comes through practice and ongoing education. Never should you believe that you are done with studying. Life is always filled with new potential, which you can only unlock when you read and comprehend new concepts. We are not meant to stay idle as life passes us by. On the contrary, we need to move along with it, evolve, and unravel the hidden mysteries ahead. Allow yourself the time to master what you have learned so far. Try out different meditations which will unlock the parts of your body, your mind, your soul. Read all about setting the right atmosphere, which will awaken the senses and allow you to relax, opening your inner self.

Accept reality for what it is, and do not ignore the facts. You have endless power for change, but this doesn't mean that you will be able to form reality exactly the way you want it from one moment to the next. The Law of Attraction doesn't work like that. You first have to change your mindset and then go ahead with receiving what you want in life. This is a huge step you need to take, so don't be impatient. Set realistic goals and build your truth, brick by brick. In this way, you will create a solid masterpiece that will not fall to pieces with the first strong wind.

No matter how many setbacks you have experienced, you should not give up. Persistence is the key to success. Even the most successful people in life have experienced failure. In fact, some of these failures have played a catalytic role in their later development. You must make use of everything you've got. Take that failure and use it to your advantage. Learn from it, so as not to make the same mistakes ever again. This is exceptional knowledge, coming straight from experience, and it will serve as your shield of protection in the future. Unless you have had a taste of failure, chances are that you will not have the chance to succeed.

If you are an athlete, think of enlightenment and your journey towards awakening your divine power as a marathon. Do you enjoy running? If you try to sprint in a marathon, eventually you will come to the realization that you are wasting your energy and you have been laboring under false pretenses. The best strategy is to preserve your energy, and stick to your end goal. Maintain your power, find your ideal pace, and make sure that you keep up with the rhythm. This is going to bring you to the finish line sooner than anticipated!

AFTERWORD

OK, now what? Are you supposed to go on with your life, like your awakening has never taken place? Now that you have had a taste of your divine power, what are you meant to do? These are questions that must be running through your mind all the time. It is perfectly understandable, since what you have experienced is a true revelation. You have been awakened. You have managed to experience what only a few women do in their life. This means that you are special and must make good use of these special traits of yours. After having discovered something as mind blowing as this, it makes sense that you feel at a loss. "Where am I going from here?", "Which is the next step I should take?" and "Is this really happening to me?" are some of the questions you need to come up with answers right away.

I totally get it; you have been overwhelmed by emotion. It is like everything in your life is beginning to make sense. You are not the insecure woman that you once were. Fear does not define you any more. On the contrary, you have realize the magnitude of power that you hold within you and it makes your heart beat faster. You are most likely finding it hard to concentrate on anything but your recent transcendental experience. By now, you have probably played the same thing over and over again in your mind, trying to discover even more details and savor every moment. I can't blame you. I was in shock when I found out about my true calling, and it took me a while to bounce back and resume my ordinary life.

Obviously, you are not expected to figure it all out from one day to the next. There is a learning curve, which you are about to follow. Every day, you will discover new things that you knew nothing about. Think of it as landing on a new planet, and trying to discover what lies out there. You cannot just start walking and walking until you have covered the entire planet, can you? That would turn out to be disastrous, as you would exhaust yourself and not have the clarity required to interpret the signs. Step by step, you must lay out your plans and figure out the best way to cover as much distance as possible each time.

This is earth shattering news that you have found; no one would be able to relax and just go out and about with their daily routine. It is impossible to go sit in front of a computer and do some data entry, or start answering the phone, without wanting to shout about your transformation. You have communicated with your inner goddess, finding just a small fraction of your power. Now you need to put this into perspective. You cannot change your life radically because it would throw you off guard. What you can do is to take baby steps, and read, and then read some more about what is happening to you. In this book, I hope I have given you the answers to all your questions, but you must continue your education for life.

It is important to stick to your routine and incorporate this immense change into your life in a way that does not mess with your reality check. Otherwise, you could be looking at social isolation. If you compare this experience to anything else you have ever lived so far, there will be a huge distance between them. However, you should not underestimate what has brought you to the place you are now. Do not forget about the people who have stood by your side. They deserve to be happy by your side, so don't exclude them from your life. On the other hand, those who have criticized and made fun of your beliefs do not belong anywhere near you.

THE WORLD IS YOUR OYSTER

...and you are the pearl. Life is full of surprises and you are ready to face the world with a different mindset. You are divine, you are sacred, you have been chosen to bless the earth and communicate with the universe. There is divinity within you, your inner goddess is inviting you to experience greatness. What is holding you back? Take that opportunity and make the most of it. Everyday should be a celebration of your unique nature. You are equipped to take on the world, pursuing your dreams and hopes until you instill life into them.

Take a look at the mirror and tell me what you see. I see an empowered woman, who is eager to discover all the hidden truths in life. You are thirsty for knowledge and you want to create, nurture, support and relish. There is nothing to stop you from your course. You are determined to survive and thrive against all odds. Your goal is to spread the word to others, letting women know just how powerful they really are. It is in your hands. You have the ability to influence more females into exploring their divine feminine power. This is your calling. This is your destiny. Enjoy being in the spotlight because you deserve it. Enjoy letting others walk in your shoes and follow your lead. You have earned it.

You are free to fly away in searches, discover uncharted lands, delve in crisp waters, and explore the vastness of the ocean. Nothing can stand in the way. It is sheer power that is guiding you, along with the enlightenment of deep knowledge from eternity. Take a look at the sun, the stars and the moon. Observe how great they are, shining on their own. They don't need anyone else to validate them. Instead, they know their true value and they never underestimate who they are. Imagine the infinite, the ancient power that has survived through millennia. You are part of this mystical truth. You are part of the universe, in perfect sync with its power.

The world is your oyster, because you are powerful and extraordinary. You are able to chart your own course, decide where you want to go and what you want to do. There is no restriction. There is no one who can deny your immense power and limitless possibilities in life. Rather than finding excuses to reject your options and narrow them down to what is familiar, you need to expand and broaden your horizons. Step out of your comfort zone. You have not come all this way to simply settle for what others dictate. On the contrary, you have always been a visionary. Never has your mind rested; you always try to learn more and discover what remains hidden in the darkness.

With the shocking revelation that you are a sacred entity, directly connected to your ancient spirit, how can you change your beliefs and live life differently? Reach out to the world, revealing your secrets and connecting to others who are experiencing the same things, as you do so. Your life is about to change more than you know. Train your brain, acknowledge the changes, and figure out how to control your inner energy. This is the pathway to true awareness. Then, you will be unstoppable. You will have the power to flow through the universe, calling out nature's most precious elements to bathe you with wisdom, love, light and hope. An ethereal creature like you is entitled to all these magnificent things in life. You just have to reach out and take what is rightfully yours. Brace yourself, because this is going to be a life-changing experience!

A Heartfelt Farewell

Congratulations, dear females! You have successfully completed your path towards enlightenment and it is time to reveal the next step. How are you moving forward with your life now that you have stepped into your divine power? Throughout the book, I have tried to describe in detail every single part of the awakening process. I know that the journey is going to be different for every single one of you ladies. However, there is one thing I can promise right here, right now. If you follow the steps that I have laid out in these sections, you will get much closer to your inner goddess than ever before. This is an accomplishment on its own.

I hope that you have already come to realize just how unique your true self is. It would be an honor for me to hear that you have appreciated your feminine side a little more, thanks to some of the things I said. You need to be aware of your special higher self and always treat yourself right. There are ways to reach deep within your soul and discover your feminine energy. Over time, you will learn how to master this flow of energy, so that you can contain it and use it exactly the way you want. This wonderful immense source of energy will offer you endless possibilities in life, so you should keep your eyes open and make use of that.

I wish you all love in life. You deserve a life filled with love and care, so make sure that you surround yourself with people who are generous. More than that, I wish you light in your life; may it bathe you with its beneficial properties. The pure light shining over you and offering you all those warm feelings comes from awareness and curiosity. I hope that this is the light that guides you through your journey. This is going to be an extraordinary experience for you. And above all, I wish you courage. There will be times when you feel like giving up. As I told you earlier in the book, awakening your feminine energy is not all roses and flowers. So you will need all the courage you can have, so as to endure the pain, and make it through the hard work and strenuous effort.

This experience will only make you stronger and more enlightened. Do not shy away from the challenge. Read through the different sections, taking in all the details that form your guiding light. This will be your beacon, even when you feel lost on your journey. Turn back to the pages that deal with specific aspects of your awakening and try to understand them. This is hard-earned knowledge, which I was lucky enough to document and pass on to you. Feel free to read again and again, until you fully perceive the concept of reaching your divine feminine. Your transformation has already begun, which is an outstanding thing to consider. This is something you should be proud of. Not many women have been blessed to live the way you do. So it is your duty to take on the challenge and make the most of it every single day.

Take a moment and contemplate what you have achieved so far. You have come a long way and I couldn't be prouder of you, girls. Now, everything is changing. Your life will improve drastically now that you have grasped the full potential of your inner power. All this empirical knowledge is available to you now that you have completed this book.

AFTERWORD

Reach out and take what you want, because your time has come. It is your moment to shine and radiate with a blissful glow, showing the world what you are made of. You are sacred. You are unique. You are wonderful. Good luck on your journey, and I wish you all the best...which I am sure you are bound to experience, now that you have completed your goddess energy awakening!

REFERENCES

Create Balance And Harmony Using The Law Of Polarity. (2016, December). www.Magzter.com. https://www.magzter.com/article/ Lifestyle/OMTimes-Magazine/Create-Balance-And-Harmony-Using-TheLaw-Of-Polarity

dc20462. (2017). Glow Woman Women. In *Pixabay*. https://pixabay. com/photos/glow-woman-women-s-silhouette-sea-2826154/

Devanath. (2016). Lotus Natural Water. In *Pixabay*. https://pixabay. com/photos/lotus-natural-water-meditation-zen-1205631/

FelixMittermeier. (2017). Milky Way Starry Sky Night. In *Pixabay*. https://pixabay.com/photos/milky-way-starry-sky-night-sky-star-2695569/

Fotorech. (2017). Sky Freedom Happiness. In *Pixabay*. https:// pixabay.com/photos/sky-freedom-happiness-relieved-2667455/

Free Photos. (2014). Summerfield Woman Girl. In *Pixabay*. https:// pixabay.com/photos/summerfield-woman-girl-sunset-336672/

Free Photos. (2015). Sparkler Holding Hands. In *Pixabay*. https:// pixabay.com/photos/sparkler-holding-hands-firework-677774/

Free Photos. (2016). Person Mountain Top Achieve. In *Pixabay*. https://pixabay.com/photos/person-mountain-top-achieve-1245959/

geralt. (2019). Self Love Heart Diary. In *Pixabay*. https://pixabay.com/photos/self-love-heart-diary-hand-keep-3969644/

Gorbachevsergeyfoto. (2018). Woman Portrait Girl. In *Pixabay*. https://pixabay.com/photos/woman-portrait-girl-people-model-3287956/

Hans. (2016). Girl Person Child Summer. In *Pixabay*. https://pixabay.com/photos/girl-person-child-summer-dress-1469748/

HNewberry. (2016). Goddess Female Pagan. In *Pixabay*. https://pixabay.com/photos/goddess-female-pagan-magic-lady-1500599/

Katerina Knizakova. (2017). Model Red Weed Field. In *Pixabay*. https://pixabay.com/photos/model-red-weed-field-green-plant-1955528/

kudybadorota. (2018). Girl Daydreaming Horse. In *Pixabay*. https://pixabay.com/photos/girl-daydreaming-horse-daydream-3551832/

Leninscape. (2017). Yoga Outdoor Woman. In *Pixabay*. https://pixabay.com/photos/yoga-outdoor-woman-pose-young-2176668/

msandersmusic. (2016). Stained Glass Spiral Circle. In *Pixabay*. https://pixabay.com/photos/stained-glass-spiral-circle-pattern-1181864/

netage. (n.d.). The Da Vinci Code & Mary Magdalene l. Netage.Org. https://netage.org/the-da-vinci-code-mary-magdalene/

NRThaele. (2017). Girl Freedom Climbing. In *Pixabay*. https://pixabay.com/photos/girl-freedom-climbing-hiking-1955797/

Paulo Coelho - Wikiquote. (n.d.). En.Wikiquote.Org. Retrieved September 15, 2020, from https://en.wikiquote.org/wiki/Paulo_Coelho

Peterson, J. (2020, March 4). *Jordan Peterson explains the yin yang symbol*. Logo Design Love. https://www.logodesignlove.com/yin-yang-symbol

Piro4d. (2017). Feng Shui Stones Coast. In *Pixabay*. https://pixabay.com/photos/feng-shui-stones-coast-spirituality-1960783/

Qimono. (2018). Drop Splash Drip. In *Pixabay*. https://pixabay.com/photos/drop-splash-drip-water-liquid-wet-3698073/

Silviarita. (2017). Young Woman Girl Umbrella. In *Pixabay*. https://pixabay.com/photos/young-woman-girl-umbrella-rain-out-2268348/

Sweetlouise. (2017). Necklace Heart Stones White. In *Pixabay*. https://pixabay.com/photos/necklace-heart-stones-white-gold-2149668/

The Law Of Attraction—Discover How to Improve Your Life. (n.d.). The Law Of Attraction. Retrieved September 15, 2020, from https://www.thelawofattraction.com/

Wikipedia Contributors. (2019, April 27). *Self-fulfilling prophecy*. Wikipedia; Wikimedia Foundation. https://en.wikipedia.org/wiki/Self-fulfilling_prophecy

GET YOUR *BONUS* MANIFESTING SECRET FORMULA TOOLKIT

Are you DONE with settling for a mediocre life, wasting precious time, & ready to live your wildest fantasies?

- Hack your brain, boost performance, & release blocks holding you back from greatness
- Awaken this amazing energy to supercharge your manifestations
- Stop wasting what little precious time you have on ineffective methods

1. **Supercharged Manifestation EFT Tapping Video**
   Download To Banish Limiting Beliefs & Propel You Toward Your Dream Life! (Infused with 432 Hz Frequency)

1. **Secret Formula Journal!** Daily manifestation Ritual Done For You, Simply Rinse & Repeat At Home! (You Can Print This Out, Stick On Your Wall, & Cross Off The Days You Complete The Ritual)

1. **Powerful 10 Minute 'Shifting Your reality' Guided Meditation** MP3 Download (Infused with 528 Hz Frequency)

1. ***BONUS*** LOA boosting 10 Minute 'Feminine Energy Awakening' Guided Meditation MP3 Download

Go To This Link To Get Your *BONUS* Manifesting Secret Formula Toolkit:

bit.ly/manifestingforwomen

PLEASE LEAVE A REVIEW ON AMAZON

From the bottom of my heart, thank you for reading my book. I truly hope that it helps you on your spiritual journey and to live a more empowered and happy life. If it does help you, then I'd like to ask you for a favor. Would you be kind enough to leave an honest review for this book on Amazon? It'd be greatly appreciated and will likely impact the lives of other spiritual seekers across the globe, giving them hope and power. I read **every** review I receive and they help me to become the best writer and spiritual teacher that I can be.

Thank you and good luck!

Angela Grace

Why not join our Facebook community and discuss your spiritual path with like-minded seekers?

We would love to hear from you!

Go here to join the 'Ascending Vibrations' community:

bit.ly/ascendingvibrations

YOUR FREE AUDIOBOOK IS READY

Download the 6+ Hour Audiobook *'Divine Feminine Energy (Manifesting for Women & Feminine Energy Awakening - 2 in 1 Collection)'* Instantly for **FREE!**

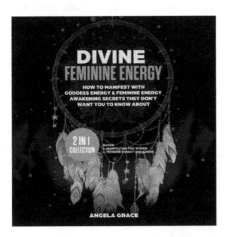

If you love listening to audio books on-the-go, I have great news for you. You can download the audio book version of *'Divine Feminine Energy'* for **FREE** just by signing up for a **FREE** 30-day audible trial! See below for more details!

Audible trial benefits

As an audible customer, you'll receive the below benefits with you 30-day free trial:

- Free audible copy of this book

- After the trial, you will get 1 credit each month to use on any audiobook
- Your credits automatically roll over to the next month if you don't use them
- Choose from over 400,000 titles
- Listen anywhere with the audible app across multiple devices
- Make easy, no hassle exchanges of any audiobook you don't love
- Keep your audiobooks forever, even if you cancel your membership
- And much more

Go to the links below to get started:

Go here for AUDIBLE US: bit.ly/divinefeminineenergy
Go here for AUDIBLE UK: bit.ly/divinefeminineenergyuk

Printed in the USA
CPSIA information can be obtained
at www.ICGtesting.com
LVHW071532131223
766027LV00005B/167